THE FESTIVAL OF SPRING FROM THE DÍVÁN OF JELÁLEDDÍN

JELÁLEDDÍN RÚMÍ

Introduction by
WILLIAM HASTIE

This Book with its Sincere
Utterances of Love and Friendship
towards the Highest
is dedicated to

WILLIAM A. SANDERSON, ESQ.

Byethorne, Galashiels
My ever faithful Friend
in Adversity, as in Prosperity

Old Songs are sweetest
Old Friends are best

CONTENTS

INTRODUCTION
I.   13
II.   25
III.   38

FIFTY GAZELS OF JELÁLEDDÍN
I. Light   61
II. Death and Life   63
III. Invocation   64
IV. Faith   67
V. Dawn   69
VI. Allah Hu!   71
VII. Spring   73
VIII. Spring's Festival   75
IX. Dependence   78
X. Mystical Union   80
XI. Identity   83
XII. Confession   85
XIII. Discordia Concors   87
XIV. Renovation   90
XV. Revolving in Mystic Dance   93
XVI. The Soul in All   95
XVII. Responsibility   98

XVIII. Action	100
XIX. Bondage	102
XX. Love's Freedom	104
XXI. In My Heart	106
XXII. Not Deaf to Love	108
XXIII. Assimilation	110
XXIV. Cleanliness	113
XXV. Where is He?	115
XXVI. Love's Slavery	117
XXVII. Psyche in Tears	119
XXVIII. Substitutional	121
XXIX. God's Throne	123
XXX. The Lion of God	125
XXXI. Self-Realisation	128
XXXII. Thy Hand!	130
XXXIII. The Priests	132
XXXIV. The Pilgrims	134
XXXV. Many Faiths, One Lord	136
XXXVI. Love Absolute	138
XXXVII. Renunciation	140
XXXVIII. All Fulness	141
XXXIX. Friendship	142
XL. The Friend Supreme	144
XLI. Immortality	147
XLII. The First and Last	149
XLIII. Mystic Love Dance	151
XLIV. Dream Fear	154
XLV. The Cry of Love	156
XLVI. Night Thought	159

XLVII. Up out of Night	161
XLVIII. All One	164
XLIX. O Wake in Me	166
L. Jeláleddín	169
NOTES.	
A. SIR WILLIAM JONES ON THE MYSTICAL POETRY OF THE PERSIANS.	173
B. HEGEL ON THE CHARACTER OF THE PERSIAN LYRICAL POETRY.	176
C. VON HAMMER'S ACCOUNT OF OMAR KHAYYÁM.	180
Also available	185

'In Depth of Conception, as well as in Loftiness of Flight and Sublimity of Language, Jeláleddín surpasses all the Poets of the East.'

— PR. HERMANN ETHÉ.

'The greatest Mystical Poet of any Age.'

— R. A. NICHOLSON.

'And all the Breeze of Fancy blows,
And every Dew-drop paints a bow,
The wizard Lightnings deeply glow,
And every Thought breaks out a Rose.'

— TENNYSON.

NOTE

The current, popular spelling of Persian Names and Words has been generally adopted in the following pages, in order to avoid any appearance of pedantry. The *Turkish* forms have occasionally been preferred when in place, *e.g. Devlet* for *Daulat*, and *Mevlānā* for *Maulānā*. The exact transliteration of the Persian—such as Jalálu-'d-Din, Shams-ud-Din, Umar, Ghasal, Díwán—will be found in the footnote references to more learned Works.

INTRODUCTION

I.

Jeláleddín Rúmí (A.D. 1207-1273) is now universally recognised by 'those who know,' as the greatest of the Persian Mystical Poets. This supremacy, in his own sphere, has been unanimously accorded to him for more than six centuries, by unnumbered myriads of his own disciples and followers in the Oriental World, who have been wrapt in devoutest admiration of the great Master to whom they have owed the highest joy and inspiration of their spiritual life. And at last, in our own Western World, the great Persian scholars of Europe, looking at him without personal or national bias, and through the clear, cold light of the new time, have come more and more, as with one voice, to join in this chorus of praise. His most appreciative recent editor and interpreter in England, in presenting a few leaves plucked with reverent hand from what he calls Jeláleddín's 'wreath of imperishable Lyric Song,' offers his own careful and conscientious work to us, as a contribution 'to a better appreciation of *the greatest mystical poet of any age.*' And with this designation, as summing up the judgment of a capable expert and critic—strange as it may sound—we venture, in all deference and sincerity, to agree. Jeláleddín is now rising upon our literary horizon in all his native Splendour—his name appropriately signifying 'The Splendour of the Faith'—as at once the Dante, the St. Bernard, the Spenser, the Milton, the Angelus Silesius, and the Novalis of the Orient. As a religious Lyrical Poet his mellifluous music, his variety of strain, his captivating charm of words, his purity of feeling, his joyous faith, and his elevation of thought, have never been surpassed in their own kind. Taking what Matthew Arnold has called 'the lyrical cry' even in its widest range, it would be doing no one wrong—although it dare hardly be done as yet—to rank Jeláleddín, when he comes fully before us 'with all his singing robes about him,' with the very highest—with Shakespeare, with Wordsworth and Keats and Shelley, and with Goethe and Heine! He is certainly one of the most fertile poets of Nature among the Lyrical Singers of all time, and the most exuberant, if not also the most spiritual, Hymnist the world outside of Christendom has yet produced.

This estimate, however shaded or qualified, cannot but appear at first strangely exaggerated, and out of all just proportion, to those who mayhap read the name of Jeláleddín now for the first time. Let us listen, then, to the greatest students of Persian Poetry in the critical Nineteenth Century, the judges who have highest authority on the subject, and who have the best right to pronounce judgment on Jeláleddín. And let us hear in the first place, as is his due, the most learned Historian of Persian Poetry in the Nineteenth Century, who with indefatigable industry and completest knowledge has adorned his pages with Extracts from no less than Two Hundred of Persia's greatest Poets. Joseph von Hammer, the great Austrian Orientalist (known later as Baron Von Hammer-Purgstall and as the Historian of Arabic Literature in seven immense volumes, containing Accounts of nearly ten thousand Authors) says:—

'Jeláleddín Rumi is the greatest Mystical Poet of the East, the Oracle of the Sofis, the Nightingale of the contemplative life, the Author of the Mesnevi (a celebrated double-rhymed ascetic poem), and the Founder of the Mevlevi, the most famous Order of Mystical Dervishes. As Founder of this Order, as the Legislator of the Contemplative Life, and as the Interpreter of Heavenly Mysteries, he is highly revered. And as such he has to be estimated by quite a different standard from that which applies to those Poets whose inspiration has not soared, like his, to the Vision of Divine things, to the primal Fountain of Love and Light. He cannot properly be compared either with Firdusi, the greatest of the Persian Epic Poets, nor with Nizami, the greatest of the Romantic Poets, nor with Saadi, the first of the moral Didactic Poets, nor with Hafiz, the chiefest of the erotic Lyrical Poets; for all these won the Palm of Poetry in entirely different fields from his. The only two great Poets of his kind, with whom a comparison can be in place, Senayi, the Author of the Mystical 'Flower Garden,' and Attar, the Author of the Mystical 'Bird Dialogues.' But both these works stand, as regards poetic merit, far below the Mesnevi, which is the Text Book of all The Sofis, from the banks of the Ganges to the shores of the Bosphorus. The Collection of Jeláleddín's 'Lyrical Poems'—his Divan, properly so called—'is regarded by them as of still higher value; it is practically the Law Book and the Ritual of all these Mystics. These outbursts of the highest inspiration of its kind deserve to be more closely considered, as it is from them that we see shining forth as in clear splendour the essence of the Oriental Mysticism, the cardinal Doctrine that All is One—the view of the ultimate Unity of all Being—and giving with it Direction and Guidance to the highest goal of Perfection by the contemplative Way of Divine Love. On the wings of the highest religious enthusiasm, the Sofi, rising above all the outward forms of positive Religions, adores the Eternal Being, in the completest abstraction from all that is sensuous and earthly, as the purest Source of Eternal Light. Mevláná Jeláleddín thus soars, not only like other Lyrical Poets, such as Hafiz, over Suns and Moons, but even above Space and Time, above the world of Creation and Fate, above the Original Contract of Predestination, and beyond the Last Judgment, into the Infinite, where in Eternal Adoration he melts into One with the Eternal Being, and infinitely loving, becomes One with the Infinite Love—ever forgetting himself and having only the great All in his view.'[1]

Thus far the learned Von Hammer. But let us also hear the judgment of the East itself, of which this is only a Western echo, as it may be gathered from Devletshah, the greatest native biographer—the Dr. Johnson we may appropriately say—of the Persian Poets. Of Jeláleddín, he says:—

'His pure Heart is filled with Divine Mysteries, and through his eradiating Soul streams the Infinite Light. His View of the World leads the thirsty in the Vale of the Contemplative Life to the refreshing Fountain of Knowledge; and his Guidance leads those who have wandered in the Wilderness of Ignorance into the Gardens where Truth is really known. He makes plain to the Pilgrim the Secrets of the Way of Unity, and unveils the Mysteries of the Path of Eternal Truth:

> *As when the foaming Sea high swells in*
> *Wave upon Wave,*
> *It casts out Pearls upon Pearls on every*
> *Shore they lave.'*

And to cite only one Turkish Authority—for the Turks claim Jeláleddín as their own, although a Persian of royal race, born at Balkh, old Bactra, on the ground of his having sung and died at Qoniya, in Asia Minor (the Iconium of Paul and Barnabas and Timothy and St. Thecla), whence he was called Rumi 'the Roman,' usually rendered 'the Greek,' as wonning within the confines of old Oriental Rome. This is how Fehîm Efendi, the Turkish Historian of the Persian Literature, himself a Poet, begins his Sketch of the Life of the great poetic Mystagogue:—

'As the ideal of Searchers after Truth here below, as the pattern of the Pure, the Mevlana is honoured by great and small among the people, by the aristocrat and the common man. In all circles his words are held in high honour; among all the wise his knowledge is greatly esteemed; and no pen has had the power to praise him, and to celebrate his excellence worthily, or to describe it in fitting terms.

> *And should the fancy hold it can*
> *His praise completely reach;*
> *Mevlana's praise it ne'er shall scan—*

THE FESTIVAL OF SPRING FROM THE DÍVÁN ... | 19

How say it then in speech?'

Rosen, who gives this quotation, and an excellent rhymed German translation of part of the Mesnevi, refers to that poem as not only 'one of the most celebrated productions of the Persian Mysticism, but as being regarded by many Mohammedans as almost equal in holiness to the Koran and the Sunna.' Being attached, at the time he wrote, to the German Embassy at Constantinople, Rosen also mentions that not only did the educated Oriental regard the Mesnevi as the most perfect Book of Edification, which when its contents were received into his mind and heart, made him certain of Salvation; but that even the poor Persian retailers of the products of their home industries, on the streets, could recite with enthusiasm long passages from the poems of Jeláleddín. We believe that this holds true to-day, more or less, of the whole Mohammedan world.[2]

But coming to more familiar names, we might gather a whole cloud of the most approved witnesses in this connection. Thus Sir William Jones, the first great Anglo-Indian Scholar, the Columbus of the new Old World of Sanskrit and Persian Literature, enters with wonderful sympathy and insight into possession of the Persian and Hindu Mystical Poetry; he refers to their great Maulavi, and his astonishing work, *The Mesnevi*; and he translates the celebrated opening passage in rhyming couplets which would not have been unworthy of Pope himself.[3] Sir William Jones did not, indeed, touch Jeláleddín's Lyrics, but he rendered some precious morsels of Hafiz, 'Odes,' as they are called, both in English and French, in a way that made young European students and poets, like Herder and Goethe, turn again to the East with yearning expectant eyes. Similar testimony might be adduced from Henry Thomas Colebrooke, one of the very greatest of the successors of Sir W. Jones. The chief Historian of Persia, and the best informed Persian scholar of his day, Sir John Malcolm (of Langholm), if less sympathetic than Sir W. Jones in his painstaking account of the Persian Mystics, gives likewise the first place to Jeláleddín.[4] And then much more definitely Sir Gore Ouseley, the first English Biographer of the Persian Poets, gives Jeláleddín due recognition in connection with the unrivalled Mesnevi.[5] The Journal of the Asiatic Society, an ever valuable Magazine of Oriental learning, and the parent of many others of its kind, has been enriched by the contributions of many enthusiastic English scholars following in the footsteps of Sir W. Jones, and it contains the earliest fragments of English translations of Jeláleddín.[6] Robert Alfred Vaughan, in his *Hours with the Mystics*, 1856, a popular, sympathetic, and still attractive work, appreciates Jeláleddín, and compares him with Angelus Silesius and Emerson, but all his knowledge of the Persian Mystic was de-

THE FESTIVAL OF SPRING FROM THE DÍVÁN ... | 21

rived from Tholuck and Sir W. Jones. At last competent scholars began to deal worthily with Jelál's poetry in English. Sir James W. Redhouse has translated the First Book of the Mesnevi in rhyming couplets, with the utmost fidelity and care; and another distinguished Persian scholar, Mr. Whinfield, the most faithful English translator of Omar Khayyám, has given an abridged version of the whole immense work, which in the Persian original contains about 70,000 lines.[7] The Mesnevi has thus come now to be pretty well known by English readers interested in the subject; and in the last edition of the *Encyclopædia Britannica*, Professor Hermann Ethé, an unquestionable authority, in his valuable Articles on Persian Literature and Jeláleddín Rumi, sums him up as 'the *greatest* Pantheistic Writer of *all* ages,' and speaks of 'his *matchless* Odes in which he soars on the wings of a genuine enthusiasm, high over Earth and Heaven, up to the Throne of Almighty God.' Be it noted, in passing, that it is at least remarkable how two such different writers as the Turkish Devlet Shah and the learned German Orientalist should both write of Jeláleddín in terms that undesignedly, but irresistibly, recall by their very superlativeness, the famous lines of Dr. Johnson on Shakespeare:—

> '*Each change of many-coloured Life he drew,*
> *Exhausted Worlds and then imagin'd new;*
> *Existence saw him spurn her bounded reign,*

And panting Time toil'd after him in vain.'

All this makes it now intelligible that the late lamented Editor of the *Encyclopædia Britannica*, Dr. W. Robertson Smith, when Professor of Arabic at Cambridge, with the fine insight of the far-seeing scholar, should have directed the attention of a young, enthusiastic student to the 'Lyrical Poetry of Jeláleddín Rumi'; and it is to the loyal devotion of this young scholar that we owe the first appearance from an English Press of a Volume of forty-eight 'Selected Poems' of Jeláleddín, in a critical Persian Text and with accurate and elegant prose renderings.[8] Mr. Reynold A. Nicholson has thus established a right to pronounce judgment on the merits of Jeláleddín, and we now listen to him with deference, and no longer with astonishment, when he deliberately characterises him as 'the *greatest* Mystical Poet of *any* Age.'

As the object of this Introduction is only to determine, in some measure, the literary interest of the Lyrical Poetry—the Díván, as it is technically called—of Jeláleddín, space need not be taken up by narrating again what is traditionally known of his Life, and it is the less necessary as excellent accounts are now easily accessible. Sir James W. Redhouse gives in somewhat abridged translation El Eflākī's interesting narrative, with its romantic wreath of legend, and its quaint anecdotes and racy sayings. Mr.

Nicholson furnishes an excellent summary. Professor Hermann Ethé's notice in the Encycl. Brit. has been already referred to, and reference may also be made to his *Morgenländische Studien*, and his popular Lecture in the Virchow-Holtzendorff Series, 1888, on 'The Mystical, Didactic, and Lyrical Poetry, and the later Literature of the Persians,' with its fine characterization, which we would fain have quoted. Rosen translates into German the Biographical Sketches of Devletshah and Jāmi. Professor E. G. Browne's recent 'Literary History of Persia,' which carries the subject down to A.D. 1000, and is undoubtedly so far the best History of Persian Literature yet produced, contains appreciative references to Jeláleddín, with a masterly account of the Sufi Mysticism; and we look forward with much interest to a comprehensive and judicial summing up of the great Mystic Poet, by this high authority upon the whole subject.[9]

---

1. Geschichte der schönen Redekünste Persiens, mit einer Blüthenlese aus zweihundert persischen Dichtern. Von Joseph von Hammer. Wien, 1818. Pp. 163-198. The petty criticism of some of Von Hammer's details has no relevancy here, and is hardly worth referring to in connection with his gigantic achievements. There are spots on the Sun!
2. Mesnevi oder Doppelverse des Scheich Mewlânâ Dschelâl-ed-dín Rumi. Aus dem Persischen übertragen von Georg Rosen. 1849.
3. Works of Sir William Jones, Vol. IV., On the Mystical Poetry of the Persians and Hindus. See Note A.

4. History of Persia. 1815. Sir John Malcolm was surprised in Persia, as Rosen was at Constantinople, by the knowledge which the common people had of the great Persian Poets. He says:—'I was forcibly struck with this fact during my residence in Persia. I found several of my servants well acquainted with the poetry of their country; and when I was at Isfahan in 1800, I was surprised to hear a common tailor that was at work repairing one of my tents, entertain his companions with repeating some of the finest of the mystical odes of Háfidz.'
5. Biographical Notices of Persian Poets, etc. 1846. A conscientious bit of work for the time, but inadequately edited, and now practically superseded.
6. One e.g. by F. Falconer (but not in the Persian form) in July, 1839.
7. The Mesnevi (usually known as the Mesneviyi Sherif, or Holy Mesnevi of Mevlānā (our Lord) Jelálu-'d-dín, Muhammed, er-Rumi). Book the First, etc., by James W. Redhouse. London, 1881.

    Masnavi i Ma'navi. The Spiritual Couplets of Maulána Jalálu-'d-dín Muhammad Rumi, Translated and abridged by E. H. Whinfield, M.A., Late of H.M. Bengal Civil Service. 2nd Ed. 1898 (with an interesting Introduction).
8. Selected Poems from the Dīvāni Shamsi Tabrīz. Edited and Translated with an Introduction, Notes, and Appendices, by Reynold A. Nicholson, M.A., Fellow of Trinity College, Cambridge. Cambridge University Press, 1898.
9. A Literary History of Persia From the Earliest Times until Firdawsí. By Edward G. Browne, M.A., M.B., Sir Thomas Adams' Professor of Arabic and sometime Lecturer in Persian in the University of Cambridge, 1902.

II.

The interest of the writer in Jeláleddín has been from the first, and all through, philosophical and theological rather than specially historical or textual. This interest was awakened in him by Hegel. In early student days, when to him as to so many then, the Hegelian Philosophy was the all in all of his thought, he was startled by the unwonted enthusiasm with which the great thinker at the climax of his severest exposition, paused to pay a warm tribute to 'the *excellent* Jeláleddín,' when he came into view in the light of the Supreme Idea of his own System.[1] This passage in Hegel, seems always to have impressed the students of his own writings, and it has been frequently referred to both by his German and English expounders. The greatest speculative Thinker of the Nineteenth Century, seems to have felt a deep satisfaction in recognising the affinity of the greatest speculative Poet of the East to his own deepest thought, while at the same time carefully distinguishing the clearer and higher form of his own conception. Nay more, although parsimonious to the utmost of his space and words, in this, the most condensed and compacted Text Book of Philosophy written in any European language since Aristotle, the stern German Dialectician in a comparatively long footnote, says he 'cannot refrain' from quoting several passages from the Poet, in order that the reader may get a clearer knowledge of his ideas; and he quotes them from Rückert's Versions, to give, at the same time, some specimens of 'the marvellous Art of the translation.' The Reader who is not acquainted with German will find Hegel's words accurately translated by the late Dr. W. Wallace, who also gives an English version of the passages quoted from Rückert, in which he says he was 'kindly helped by Miss May Kendall'—although Dr. Wallace and Miss May, rhyming in utter ignorance of Persian Prosody, and consequently, like so many more, in the dark, have entirely failed to catch the delicate play of the Gazels, so faithfully reproduced by the tuneful Rückert.[2]

In another of Hegel's works—his valuable posthumous 'Lectures on the Philosophy of Art'—he takes up the same subject from the æsthetic point of view, and he deals with it again in a more popular, but in an essentially identical, way.[3] As the former passage has now obtained currency in our philosophical literature, it may be more useful, as well as more relevant to these pages, to reproduce the latter, the fuller and more intelligible, but hitherto untranslated, exposition. Hegel is here dealing with the Symbolical Forms of Art, and in particular with the symbolism of Sublimity, historically characteristic of Oriental Art, which thus gives expression to the consciousness of absolute subordination and the dependence of all that is individual and finite on the Universal and the Infinite. In his comprehensive historical survey Hegel, at this stage, finds occasion to deal with what he calls 'Pantheism in Art.' The profound thinker, with a vigorous grasp and original view of the historic evolution, is here singularly lucid and suggestive, as he delineates the Pantheistic Poetic Idea exhibited in the lyrical forms of 1. Indian Poetry; 2. Mohammedan Poetry; 3. Christian Mysticism. Very refreshing and sane is his representation of Indian Poetry, at a time when the uncritical enthusiasm of the Schlegels and other young Sanskrit Students, was carrying an unrestrained admiration beyond all reasonable bounds. Hegel castigates this juvenile weakness with a firm hand. He, too, has read the startling translations of the Sakuntala and the Bhagavad Gita, and he knows something of the Ramayana; but he is not dazzled or carried away. He recognises the marvellous exuberance and profusion of the Indian imagination, but it is all too fantastic as yet. While it is boundless, it is also formless, and just so far is it lacking in true Beauty. Its Sublimity is confused, chaotic, helpless; it ever struggles for a harmonious unity, for spiritual mastery of the manifold and the overwhelming, which it never attains. All this is truest insight, soundest criticism.—But a higher stage is reached in the *Persian* Poetry. Here the form of the Poet becomes more adequate, more masterful, more refined. Beauty springing up with Sublimity, is harmoniously wedded with it, and in one great Poet the victory of Love is freely consummated; for—to paraphrase with Tennyson—

> *'For all the past of Time reveals*
> *A bridal dawn of thunder-peals,*
> *Wherever Thought hath wedded Fact.'*

But let us hear Hegel's own grave, well-weighed judgment, as he spoke it in those days to his own Students at Berlin:

'In a higher and subjectively freer way, the Oriental Pantheism has been developed in Mohammedanism, especially by the Persians. A special relationship now comes in. The Poet longs to behold the Divine in all things, and he actually does so behold it; but he also now surrenders his own Self and gives himself up to it, while he at the same time in the same degree grasps the Immanence of the

Divine in his own inner Being, when thus expanded and freed. And thereby there grows in him that cheerful inwardness, that free joy, that abounding blessedness which is peculiar to the Oriental, who in becoming liberated from his own individual limitations, sinks forthwith into the Eternal and Absolute, and recognises and feels in everything the Image and the Presence of the Divine. Such a consciousness of being permeated by the Divine and of a vivified, intoxicated life in God, borders on Mysticism. Above all others Jeláleddín Rumi is to be celebrated in this connection, of whose poetry Rückert has furnished us with some of the finest specimens, in which, with his marvellous power of expression, he even allows himself to play, in the most skilful and free manner, with words and rhymes, as the Persians similarly do. Love to God, with whom Man identifies his Self through the most unlimited self-surrender, and Whom, as the One, he now beholds in all the realms of space, leads him to refer and carry back all and everything to God; and this Love here forms the centre which expands on all sides and into all regions.'[4]

Hegel thus deliberately gives Jeláleddín an eminent place not only among the great Poets, but among the great Thinkers of the world. He is more than satisfied with Rückert as a translator, and he is virtually at one with Jeláleddín's principle of thought. His qualification is historical rather than essential;

the relation to Pantheism is the particular limiting condition of Jeláleddín's stage of development and environment; it is not a ground of reproach, nor of condemnation as more than relatively untrue, or rather incomplete. And so Hegel is at pains to vindicate the poet-thinker from the vulgar and unjust stigma commonly implied in the ascription of Pantheism. This he does in his remarks on the contributions to the subject by Dr. Tholuck, who became afterwards the eminent evangelical theologian of Halle, but who was then just entering on his distinguished career. Tholuck had quite a genius for languages, and his first intention was to devote himself to Oriental Philology. He prosecuted the study of Arabic, Persian and Turkish, with great zeal and success under the distinguished Dietz; and in 1821, at the age of twenty-two, he qualified as a University Teacher, by a learned Latin Dissertation on 'Sufism, or the Pantheistic Theosophy of the Persians.'[5] This remarkable exposition was at once recognised as of real merit, and it is still valuable. Tholuck, who was a born poet and had a rare breadth of literary appreciation, supplemented his work, four years later, by a very interesting Anthology from the Persian Mystical Poets in German verse, with an attractive introduction to the whole subject.[6] With the profoundest admiration for Dr. Tholuck's work as a theologian, and an unfading personal affection, kindled by tender and memorable student contact with him in his old age, we yet cannot dissent from Mr.

Whinfield's critical judgment when he thus sums up the value of these contributions: 'Tholuck was an indifferent Persian Scholar, and many of his translations are wrong, but he grasped the meaning of Sufism and its affinity to European mysticism much more thoroughly than many who were far superior to him in mere verbal scholarship.' Hegel, who was not a Persian scholar, is generous in his recognition of Tholuck's Anthology, but he points out the weakness of Tholuck's criticism, and shews in particular that the young theologian is too perfunctory in his view of the subject generally, as merely adopting the 'current chatter about Pantheism,' and hurling it as a convenient term of reproach against the whole speculative thought of the time. This shallow popular criticism, as Hegel puts it, quite misunderstands the real principle of speculative Pantheism, confounds it with a crude view of the world which immediately identifies the object of sense with the Divine, but which no sane thinker ever really held, and it is to be rejected emphatically when applied to Jeláleddín. For, as he says, 'In the excellent Jeláleddín Rumi in particular we find the unity of the soul with the One set forth, and that unity described as Love; and this spiritual unity is an exaltation above the finite and common, a transfiguration of the natural and spiritual in which the externalism and transitoriness of nature is surmounted: in *this* poetry, which soars over all that is external and sensuous, who would recognise the prosaic ideas current about so-called Pantheism?' No; Jelál is not to be tabooed, off-hand, and labelled merely as a Pantheist!

With Hegel's correction of Tholuck and his vindication of the speculative standpoint of the Persian Poet, we are entirely agreed; but Hegel is himself here not quite adequate. All students of philosophy know that in this very relation has lain the chief ambiguity and weakness of his own System, and it is reflected in his view of Jeláleddín. With his dominating passion for systematising the evolution of History and conforming it to a logical scheme of thought, he yet fails to see—largely owing to the limitation of his material—how practically modern and how spiritually personal Jelál really is. For, after all, Jeláleddín is no mere idle dreamy mediaeval Mystic; he *is* essentially a modern poet and thinker, and is *not* to be pushed back into the dim vagueness and impersonal materialism of ancient thought. He has twelve centuries of Christian life and reflection behind him, with all the dogmatic development of the ancient orthodox Church, on the one hand; all the forms of Indian pantheistic and Greek free-thought on the other; and six centuries of austere restraining Mohammedan Monotheism as his central curb and check—and well and clearly he knows them all. He is at once universally eclectic and originally constructive, and he moves freely and joyously with a larger insight all his own. The East and the

West meet in him again, more richly than they have done in any other for centuries, and he binds them into a new, happy harmony, the 'heavenly harmony' of poesy. He is a true Seer, like his own ancient Zarathustra, like Lao-tse, like Buddha, and much more akin to Jesus, and Paul, and John, than to the fierce, relentless, one-sided Prophet of Arabia, whose barren religion he redeems from its mechanical inhumanity and quickens with the breath of a purer and Diviner love. His intellectual kinship is with Plato and the speculative Theologians of the Christian Church, and with the deep dreamers who live in the highest vision and lose themselves sweetly and gladly in God. He is the veritable Morning Star of the new Day of the World, rising in pure brightness, afar in the East—and after barbaric crusade and mad war, heralding, in a clearer and sweeter Song of Divine Love, the triumph of the new time.

> *And the Nightingale thought, 'I have sung*
> *   many songs,*
> *But never a one so gay,*
> *For he sings of what the world will be*
> *When the years have died away'!*

In the year of Jeláleddín's death Edward I. ascended the throne of England, with the first faltering grasp of a mightier Empire; the boy Dante was catching the gleam of strange Visions in the shining eyes of the sweet-faced gentle maiden Beatrice; the mystic thrill that had run through the Middle Age was pulsing in the youth of Meister Eckhart, and preparing for Suso and Ruysbroek and Thomas à Kempis, through the mellifluous Rhythm of St. Bernard which had been sung for a hundred years; the Doctor Angelicus had all but summed up the system of Christian Theology, the well-worn pen just trembling to its fall from his wearied grasp; and the spirit of Martin Luther, whom of all religious Reformers Jeláleddín most resembles, was already beginning to breathe in William Occam and the free young thinkers of the time. Yes; Jeláleddín has both a wider relationship and a more modern significance than even Hegel has thought of.

And now we have surely cited Authorities enough to enable us to form at least a preliminary judgment, fair, reasonably informed, and impartial, concerning Jeláleddín's distinctive position and work as a Poet. We have seen him thrice crowned—in the Realms of Poetry, Philosophy, and Religion—by authoritative representatives, qualified kingmakers; and hardly any one who now knows truly of him, will dispute his right to be ranked as one of 'the great of old! The dead but sceptred sovrans who still rule our spirits from their urns.' His royal Title was proclaimed long ago in the musical name most aptly bestowed upon him when he lived and sang, and by those who knew him best: Jeláleddín, which we have already rendered literally as 'The Splendour of the Faith,' but which we prefer now to reproduce in its proper English equivalent as 'The Glory of Religion.' This designation at once strikingly expresses the Secret of his Power, the Consecration of his Genius, and the essence and end of his Humanity. To him Religion was all in all; it was the very Life-breath of his Soul; the Home and Joy of his Heart; the be-all and end-all of his Will. Of but very few others of the Sons of Men can this be said; of only One can it be said in a higher degree than of Jeláleddín, as he himself knew and confessed. He too 'sought for the healing Hand of Jesus,' and it purged his inner sight and enabled him to see all the world again, lying bright and beautiful, in the Light and Love of God. And moved by that all-compelling Law whose 'seat is the Bosom of God' and whose 'voice is the Harmony of the world,' he burst spontaneously into song, and the keynote of all his singing—exultant, jubilant, triumphant—was ever the living, loving God, 'Him first, Him last, Him without end.' Religion was the golden Thread on which, all his silvery poetic Pearls were strung, and he flung them around him in his own generous, selfless joy, with the most lavish hand. They seem to have cost him no effort of search or toil. Much more than Spinoza or Novalis was he a 'God-intoxicated man'; the prophetic fire burned in his soul, without consuming it and it must out in 'thoughts that breathe and words that burn.'

And this is still our precious inheritance from him to-day, which we will do well to appreciate and cherish anew in this cold, heartless, irreligious, prosaic time. Let his ringing voice then be reverently heard even through these few, faint, far-off re-echoings of his own soul-stirring elevating strains; for the burden of all he sings, in endless variation of note and tune, his one theme as he himself caught it direct from the melody of Nature and of Man, is the Glory of Religion!

This very general Introduction to the subject-matter of Jelál's Lyrics must here suffice, as our immediate object is merely to present some specimens of them in a form at once popular and generally intelligible. But the detail of the subject in its historical, philosophical and theological bearings, which would only be confusing here, is reserved for some subsequent discussion. Sir William Jones gave a first popular Epitome of the Mystical System of the Persian Poets, which in its own way has never been surpassed (see Note A), although the subject has been much more profoundly studied and elucidated since his time. A competent discussion of the system of 'the greatest Sufic poet of Persia' (Ethé), would be a valuable contribution to our contemporary Philosophy of Religion. Mr. Nicholson has concisely sketched the parallelism between the doctrines of Jeláleddín and Plotinus, but we must go further and even deeper than Plotinus in order to reach the root of the whole matter. Professor Browne is very helpful, and gives the best Literature, as also does Hughes in his most interesting illustrated Articles; Kremer is invaluable, as also are Professor Palmer on the one hand, and the recent translators and expounders of the early Iranian and Hindu Religion and Philosophy on the other; Whinfield gives an able, lucid Sketch.

---

1. Hegel's Encyklopädie der philosophischen Wissenschaften im Grundrisse. § 573. Werke, Bd. VII, 461.
2. Wallace's Hegel's Philosophy of Mind translated. Oxford, 1894, p. 190.—The four Gazels from which Hegel quotes, are given in the following Series in the Rückert-Persian form—as XLVIII, XII, XLIII, II.
3. As regards Hegel's Philosophy of Art generally, and the particular point under consideration, reference may be allowed to my little book: 'The Philosophy of Art, by Hegel and C. L. Michelet,' 1886. See especially pp. 94-6.
4. Hegel's Werke, X, 473. For Hegel's view of the character of the Persian Lyrical Poetry, see note B. M. Bénard's French Translation, which has been much praised, gives the passage quoted above, only in a summary form, and in it the reference to Rückert is entirely left out. He too, like so many other translators, has the happy knack of slipping over a troublesome phrase at times, while gracefully flourishing an elegant sentence before the delighted eyes of his guileless Reader!
5. Sufismus sive Theosophia Persarum Pantheistica quam ex MSS. Persicis, Arabicis, Turcicis, fruit atque illustravit F. A. G. Tholuck. 1821.
6. Blüthensammlung aus der Morgenländischen Mystik, nebst einer Einleitung über Mystik überhaupt und Morgenländische insbesondere. Von F. A. G. Tholuck, Professor zu Berlin. 1825.

III.

Looking now at the *poetical form* of Jelál's Lyrics, it goes without saying that it is distinctively Persian, and always eminently so in its kind. The Persian Poets were truly 'makers'; they not only created most of the nature-imagery still current in all modern poetry, but they constructed new forms of rhythm and rhyme, in which they finely echoed the sweetest melodies of nature and gave a richer and more expressive music to human speech. Their fluent and flexible language, with its natural wealth of resonant cadences and rhymes, furnished them with a facile medium of expression, and the still richer Arabic readily lent its copious resources at need. And the Persians were always rhyming, in public and private, on great themes or small; a poetic people, ever ready to recognise and honour sweet songsters; the readiest

THE FESTIVAL OF SPRING FROM THE DÍVÁN ... | 39

and wittiest of 'improvvisatori.' Even yet, as Richardson tells us; 'it is a common entertainment for the great and learned men in Persia, to assemble together, with the view to an exercise of genius, in the resolving of enigmas ... and to rival one another in the facility of composing and replying to extempore verses, in which, from practice and a natural liveliness of fancy, many of them arrive at an astonishing proficiency.' Hence, as Goethe says of himself, the Persian Poets 'sang as the birds sing;' and taking that master-singer of Nature, the Nightingale, as their model, they too trilled in strains of unrivalled sweetness, range and depth of tone, and consummate florid beauty. Even the most careless reader cannot fail to be impressed by the affluence of imagery in the Persian Lyrical Poetry, and no one has dwelt more suggestively than Hegel on the spiritual significance of its characteristic profusion of metaphors, images, similes, and comparisons.[1] But while so lavishly employing the decorative forms common to all lyrical poetry, the Persian Poets, with singular constructive originality, also created new lyrical forms of their own, and carried them to their highest perfection. Chief of these are the *Gazel* and the *Divan*, two terms which are only now being naturalised in our language, and becoming generally understood. Here, again, it may be more serviceable to quote one or two authorities, rather than to give a mere abstract definition; and as we have generally found the *older* authorities in these matters to be the best, we start with Richardson's summary of the definitions of D'Herbelot and Revizky.

'The Ghazel or Eastern Ode—says Richardson—is a species of poem, the subject of which is in general *Love* and *Wine*, interspersed with moral sentiments, and reflections on the virtues and vices of mankind. It ought never to consist of less than 5 *beits* or distichs, nor exceed 18, according to D'Herbelot; if the poem is less than five, it is then called *rabat* or quartain; if it is more than eighteen, it then assumes the name of *kasside* or elegy. Baron Revizky[2] says, that all poems of this kind which exceed 13 *beits* [couplets], rank with the *kasside*; and, according to Meninski, the ghazel ought never to have more than 11.—Every verse in the same *ghazel* must rhyme with the same letter; and when a poet has completed a *series* of such poems (the rhymes of the first class being in *alif* [a], the second in *be* [b], and so on through the whole alphabet), it is called a *Divan*, and he obtains the title of *Hafez*, or as the Arabians pronounce it, *Hafedh*.... The *ghazel* is more irregular than the Greek or Latin Ode, one verse having often no apparent connection either with the foregoing or subsequent couplets. Ghazels were often, says Baron Revizky, written or spoken *extempore* at banquets or public festivities, when the poet, after expressing his ideas in one distich, impatient of confinement, roved through the regions of fancy, as wine or a luxuriant imagination inspired.'[3]

This is excellent, and thoroughly intelligible. But let us take from Rückert's most learned work, the more authoritative concise statement of the 'Heft Kolzum': 'The Ghazel is a poem of several Beits, which have all one measure and one rhyme. According to some, there should not be more than 11 Beits, according to others 12; but some are found having as many as 19.'[4]

The term Gazel has now secured its place in our great Dictionaries, and none gives it better than Professor Whitney's New York 'Century Dictionary': 'Gázel (also Ghazal, Pers. *ghazal*, Ar. *ghazel*, *ghazal*, a Love Poem). In Persian Poetry, a form of verse in which the two first lines rime, and for this rime a new one must be found in the second line of each succeeding couplet, the alternate line being free.'— Dr. Murray's Oxford New English Dictionary defines thus: 'A species of Oriental lyric poetry, generally of an erotic nature, distinguished from other forms of Eastern verse by having a limited number of Stanzas, and by the recurrence of the same rhyme.' And most concise of all, Funk's Standard Dictionary: 'A Persian lyric poem, amatory ode, drinking song, or religious hymn, having alternate verses riming with the first couplet.' 'The *ghazel* consists usually of not less than five, or more than fifteen Couplets, all with the same rhyme.'—W. R.

Alger, Poetry of the East, p. 66.—Before leaving the Dictionaries, be it noted briefly, that the word *gházăl* (originally Arabic, and to be distinguished from *gházāl*, a young Fawn, *our* Gazelle, through the French), derived from a root signifying to *spin*, means in Persian, a thing *spun, twined, twisted*, as out of a thread; and so it designates an ode, a short poem, a sonnet' (Steingass), 'never exceeding 18 distichs, nor less than 5, *the last line of every couplet ending with the same Letter in which the first distich rhymes.*' (Richardson's Persian, Arabic and English Dictionary, *s.v.*).

All this is surely enough to elucidate the form and structure of the Persian *ghazel*, but we may further quote a completing phrase or two from that conscientious and much lamented Oriental Scholar, Mr. E. J. W. Gibb, who has treated it most fully and accurately in his valuable works on Ottoman Poetry. The Ghazel, he says, is 'the most typically Oriental of all the verse-forms alike in the careful elaboration of its detail and in its characteristic want of homogeneity. It is a short poem of not fewer than four and not more than fifteen couplets. Such at any rate is the theoretical limit, but Ghazels containing a much larger number of couplets may occasionally be met with; this, however, is exceptional, from five to ten being the average number.... If we employ the alphabetical notation usually adopted when dealing with rhyme sequences, we get the following for a Ghazel of six couplets: A.A : B.A : C.A : D.A : E.A : F.A.... In point of style the poem should be faultless; all imperfect rhymes, uncouth words questionable expressions must be carefully avoided, and the same rhyme-word ought not to be repeated. It is the most elegant and highly finished of all the old poetic forms.... Hence perhaps the extraordinary popularity of the form.... What the sonnet was to the Italian, the Ghazel was to the Persians and Turks.'[5]

This will surely suffice to explain the structure and laws of the Gazel. The Shakesperian Sonnet comes nearest its form in our poetical versification, and can by comparatively slight modification be adapted to it. Imagine the final rhyming couplet of such a sonnet placed first, and the same rhyme carried on through each of the succeeding couplets in the alternate even-numbered lines, 4, 6, 8, 10, 12, while the other odd lines (3, 5, etc.) are left unrhymed, and we would have a regular Gazel which, however, might extend to 18 couplets in all. Or, taking another familiar instance: let the Quatrain, as in Fitzgerald's 'Omar Khayyám,' be *extended* by adding further couplets (within the limits laid down) to the *second* couplet, all corresponding to it in form and rhyme, and the Quatrain passes into a regular Gazel. The Fifty examples here given are all in regular form within legitimate variation, and the structure and rhyme in any of them may be seen at a glance, even in those with an added recurring refrain in such as were generally adapted to accompany mystic dancing. Simple as the structure of the Gazel itself is, it is practically more difficult to construct it in English than in Persian, from its relative paucity of suitable rhymes.

To Rückert belongs the unfading distinction of having introduced the original form of the Ghazel into European Literature. For this achievement he was particularly qualified by his poetic gift and his deft power of artistic adaptation. An enthusiastic and loyal pupil of Von Hammer, he soon surpassed his master by the greater accuracy of his scholarship, his finer and deeper insight, and his unrivalled power of sympathetically reproducing in German the spirit of Oriental Poetry. His renderings of certain Gazels of Jeláleddín in 1819 and 1822 are masterpieces of their kind in the fineness and delicacy of their form, and they have never been equalled by similar subsequent attempts. The highest praise that Mr. Nicholson can bestow on the later excellent contribution in German of other 75 of Jelál's Ghazels by Von Rosenzweig, the accomplished translator of Hafiz, is 'that we are occasionally reminded of Rückert'; and, strangely enough, Mr. Nicholson makes no other allusion to Rückert. Rückert, whose many wonderful feats of this kind not only from Persian, but from Arabic, Sanskrit, and even Chinese, are beyond all praise, was quite conscious both of the success and importance of his effort, as is evident from the four lines on 'The Form of the Gasel' which he prefixed to his Versions of Jelál's Gasels, which may be rendered thus:—

> *The new Form which I first, here in thy*
> * Garden plant,*
> *May, Fatherland, enrich the Garland of thy*
> * clime;*
> *And in my steps may Poets, of happy*
> * power ne'er scant,*
> *Sing true in Persian Gazel, as erst in alien*
> * rhyme.*

Rückert's example and encouragement have not been ineffective in German Literature. Besides his own original Gazels addressed to his distinguished teacher Von Hammer, Platen with a poetic versatility and elegance of form scarcely inferior to his own, Paul Heyse, and others have written excellent German Gazels, and the form is now quite naturalised in German Literature. But it is still practically an exotic in the domain of English verse. One of the first and best regular Gazels in English known to the writer, was done into English rhyme by Archbishop Trench, who represents it as by Dschelaleddin (*sic*), but it is really only an imitation of one of Rückert's Versions. Some of the recent translators of Hafiz—especially Mr. H. Bicknell—have given elegant translations of some of his

Gazels, in proper form.[6] Mr. Nicholson, notwithstanding his disbelief in the adequacy of English verse-renderings, has given two exemplary specimens in an Appendix. The Fifty Gazels here presented in English have been all done after Rückert's versions, of which they are really renderings— as indicated on the Title Page. Even when the translator felt tempted to conform more literally in some minor details to the Persian original, or fancied he could do so, he invariably returned to Rückert's form, his admiration for Rückert's judgment and art having overcome all hesitation. To Rückert, then, belongs any merit found in these free imitations of Jeláleddín; to the translator must be attributed any defect in his attempt to follow, always *longo intervallo*, the traces of the footsteps of these two great Masters. Rückert alone has been able to do justice to the poetic form and thought of Jeláleddín, and it may be deemed as daring to try to imitate Rückert as to copy the Original itself. But the attempt, even where it fails, will be most readily forgiven by the Persian scholars who best know the difficulties that have to be overcome on both sides. What is here presented is but a slight endeavour to popularise, after a holiday excursion into long-loved fields, their own much more important work, and mayhap to win a wider, well-deserved interest for it. The child who strays through the Flower Garden, will, as by irresistible impulse, pluck some of its fairest blossoms here and there, and if twined together and offered to the strong hand that cultivated and reared them, they will hardly fail to be recognised as an offering of gratitude and affection, and to be accepted with a kindly, indulgent smile.

It is beautifully related in 'Attar's Biographies of the Sufi Mystics and Saints,' that the sweet-soul'd, God-absorb'd Rábia—the Saint Teresa and Madame Guyon of Persia—was once asked: 'Dost thou hate the Devil?' '*No!*' she replied. And they asked: 'Why not?' '*Because*,' said she, '*my love to God leaves me no time to hate him.*'[7] We confess, however, that we *have* hated this new-patch'd Omar Khayyám of Mr. Fitzgerald, and have even at times been tempted to scorn the miserable, self-deluded, unhealthy fanatics of his Cult. But when we have looked again into the shining face and the glad eyes of Jeláleddín, 'the Glory of Religion,' our hate has passed into pity and our scorn into compassion. In the light of that bright Vision we cannot pause—we have 'no time' nor inclination for it—to deal, as it deserves, with this latest literary craze and delusion. The Persian Scholars have been amazed, and earnest Critics who still believe in the spiritual purpose of Poetry, have been distressed by this infatuation of the young free English mind, whose issue can only be the humiliation of convicted ignorance, spurious idolatry, and vain remorseful regret after the mad midnight debauch. All that is highest and noblest and truest in manhood is not to be thus wilfully flung away for nothing, or to be foolishly bartered for the smart Epigrams of the rudest wit and shallowest reflection. Mr. Fitzgerald by clever tailoring has indeed clothed his Satan in the well-fitting robes of an Angel of Light so that he might 'seduce, if it were possible, the very Elect,'—but for *them* all in vain do such 'lean and flashy songs, grate on their scrannel pipes of wretched straw.' He has not hesitated even to eke out his vapid pessimistic song with verses of his own, and to make his poor old Omar's voice more cracked, querulous and quavering than it ever really was. And he has therefore rightly enough separated his Bacchanalian Rhymster from the holy Choir of the sweet-voiced Persian Songsters who ever made all the grove vocal with devout praise of God. Mr. Fitzgerald's Omar—he himself declares—is not a Sufi poet at all; he is but an old tipsy toper, whose drink is literally and really that of Bacchus; and he drinks—and *drinks*!—and *drinks*! till we hear him snore even in broad day, and till his dimm'd eyes and fuddled brain cannot distinguish the plainest things even in the clearest light. With Fitzgerald's hero it is the old, sad story over again; it is *drinking—not deep thinking at all*!—that has brought him to this. Surely we know the 'Astronomer Poet' quite well now. M. Nicolas, and still better, Mr. Whinfield, have given us his own Persian Quatrains, and Mr. Payne has translated them best of all; but Edward Fitzgerald has turned them into a strange haunting music of his own, and in his hands the Astronomer Poet becomes *really* what our gifted friend Mr. Coulson Kernahan has so graphically and terribly depicted: A Literary Gent, A Study in Vanity and Dipsomania! Who cares now for his senile scepticism, his pessimistic whine, his withered cynicism, his agnostic blindness and despair, his insolent misanthropy, his impotent blasphemies? We know it all too well; it is only the work of shattered nerves, a muddled brain, and irreligious self-dissipation. See how the Astronomer Poet staggers along to his watch-tower, with that tell-tale nose and flushed brow! How his trembling hands fumble as he vainly tries to focus the stars! How his bleared eyes can find neither Zenith nor Azimuth, Algol nor Aldeboran, nor the Pointers, nor the Pole Star; and how impudently he swears in his blindness, that he too has swept through the Heavens and found *no God*! that man is but a 'Pot *of Clay*,' without freedom and without hope! and that all the World is bitter and hollow and bad! *Great Thinker*, forsooth! Well and truly does he himself say that he was 'never *deep* in anything but—*Wine*'!

But Mr. Fitzgerald protests that while Omar was not a Mystic, but only a Bacchanalian Poet, and 'that while the Wine Omar celebrates is simply the Juice of the Grape, he *bragged* more than he drank of it.' But this surely is to make him worse morally than the poor will-broken, self-abandoned drunkard! Yet after all, the excuse of 'the moderate drinker' is never quite to be trusted, as Mr. Fitzgerald himself in this case only too fully proves. The 'Tavern' too is a literal Tavern, and his very first presentation of his Hero introduces him to us crying for fresh air at cock-crow, after the night's carouse, and his kindred thirsty votaries shouting from the outside to get in:

> *'And, as the Cock crew, those who stood before*
> *The Tavern shouted*—*"Open then the Door!"'*

We soon find that he has only one fixed Article in his Creed—the *certainty* of Annihilation:

> *'One thing at least is certain*—*This Life flies;*
> *One thing is certain and the rest is Lies;*
> *The Flower that once has blown for ever dies.'*

The *only* thing here *certain* however, is that this, according to all Persian Prosody, is a *bad*, illegitimate Quatrain, and Omar himself would never have rhymed it thus! And notwithstanding these 'brave words,' it seems almost certain that the poor soul of the 'Astronomer Poet' did not entirely die out with his last unsavoury breath; for is there not the strongest *internal* evidence—and pray, mark it well, in these days of the Higher Criticism—that it was

THE FESTIVAL OF SPRING FROM THE DÍVÁN ... | 51

Omar Redivivus, in an ill-starred, yet most sincere and loveable Rustic Bard of our own, who sang gloriously at the same psychological moment, with his own boon-companions, after seven centuries of world-wide drinking, again:

> *'It is the moon,* I ken her horn,
> *That's blinkin' in the lift sae hie;*
> *She shines sae bricht to wyle us hame,*
> *But by my sooth she'll wait a wee!*
> *We are na fou, we're no that fou,*
> *But just a drappie in our ee;*
> *The* Cock *may craw, the day may daw,*
> *And aye we'll taste the barley bree!'*

We are sorry to believe, notwithstanding Mr. Fitzgerald's rather lame and halting Apology, that it became, more and more, a confirmed habit; and that 'willy-nilly' the old Nature-tyrant had it out with him too. Alas! that it should so often be so with these genial poetic souls-poets, who in their youth 'begin in gladness, and thereof in the end doth come Despondency and Madness'! In vain does the much-admired Translator protest; for again he shows poor parched old Khayyám 'by the Tavern Door *agape*'!; the Nightingale only pipes to him 'Wine! Wine! Wine!'; his burden of Clay 'with long Oblivion is gone *dry*'!; his last hope and only prayer is: 'Ah, with the Grape my fading Life provide, And *wash the Body* whence the Life has died'; and his last word and the final horror is—'an *empty* Glass!' But he is much more candid in his 'cups' than his ingenious Translator, as all such are wont at a certain stage to be; for he quite frankly tells us his Rule of Life: 'Drink!—for once dead you never shall return!' Nay, he takes us, in the most friendly way and with irresistible candour, into his most intimate confidence, and informs us how and when, and how deliberately, when he found out 'the sorry Scheme of Things,' his glorified new Creed and boasted new Life came about:—

> *'You know, my Friends, with what a brave*
>   *Carouse*
> *I made a Second Marriage in my house;*
> *Divorced old barren Reason from*
>   *my Bed,*
> *And took the Daughter of the Vine to*
>   *Spouse!'*

And what *possibly* could come of it, but what *did* come? When it could no longer be disputed that the Day *was* dawning, *then* the Reckoning *must* be settled, and his last leering grin is for his drunken boon-companions, now alas! ignominiously low:—

> *'Landlady, count the lawin',*
> *The Day is near the dawin';*
> Ye're a' blind drunk, boys,
> And I'm but jolly fou.

> *Hey tutti, taiti,*
> *How tutti, taiti—*
> Wha's fou now?'

O ye self-blinded, neurotic Votaries of the Omar Khayyám Cult, be warned in time: for be sincerely assured that on counting 'the lawin', Paying the Reckoning will be all that you will ever get, even at your drunkest, out of this bankrupt, blustering, purblind Braggart!

To crown all his fatal Candour, Omar insists, as with a sigh of vain regret, on most truly telling us his own callous judgment of it all, seeing some faint inextinguishable spark of Conscience still remained in him, as in the Ancient Mariner:—

> *'Indeed the Idols I have loved so long*
> *Have done my credit in this World much*
>   *wrong:*
> *Have* drown'd my Glory in a
>   shallow Cup
> And sold my Reputation for a song!'

So, too, with Edward Fitzgerald, who, with consummate skill, has here played the part of 'Mr. Sludge, the Medium' to perfection. And we only wish that Robert Browning, in his Berserker rage over the painful betrayal of what was dearest to him in life, had 'spit' *this*, and not what he frantically did, 'in his face' as it burst from him in scorn of one who confessed:—

> *'I cheated when I could,*
> *Rapped with my toe-joints, set sham hands*
>   *at work!...'*
> *'Indeed the Idols I have loved so long*
> *Have done my credit in this World much*
>   *wrong:*
> *Have drown'd my Glory in a*
>   *shallow Cup*
> *'R-r-r ... Cowardly scamp!*
> *I only wish I could burn down the*
>   *house,*
> *And spoil your sniggering.'*[8]

But no! we have 'no time' to waste in hating even this dram-drinking, drivelling, droning Dotard. For hark!—'That strain I heard was of a higher mood'! Its very first note 'laps us in Elysium,' and we at once forget man's self-inflicted misery and all his morbid diseases and cares—'Do I wake or sleep?'...

> *... 'Tender is the Night,*
> *And haply the Queen-Moon is on her*
>   *throne,*
> *Cluster'd around by all her starry Fays;*
> *But here there is no Light*
> *Save what from Heaven is with the breezes*
>   *blown*

THE FESTIVAL OF SPRING FROM THE DÍVÁN ... | 55

*Through verdurous glooms and winding
  mossy ways.
I cannot see what Flowers are at my feet,
Nor what soft Incense hangs upon the
  boughs,
But, in embalmèd darkness, guess each
  sweet
Wherewith the seasonable Month endows
The grass, the thicket, and the fruit-tree
  wild;
White hawthorn and the pastoral eglantine;
Fast fading violets covered up in leaves;
And mid-May's eldest child
The coming musk-rose full of dewy wine,
The murmurous haunt of flies on summer
  eves....
Thou wast not born for death, immortal
  Bird!
No hungry generations tread thee down;
The Voice I heard this passing Night was
  heard
In ancient days by Emperor and clown;
Perhaps the self-same song that found
  a path
Through the sad heart of Ruth, when, sick
  for home,
She stood in tears amid the alien corn;
The same that oft-times hath
Charm'd magic-casements, opening on
  the foam*

> *Of perilous seas, in faery lands forlorn.'*

Yes; that is surely the sweetest, the tenderest, the heavenliest of all the Persian Nightingales, come back to us in our sorest need, and singing to us amid the glory of the Resurrection of Life, in the Festival of another Spring, as he never sang in the English air before. It is a Western youthful Poet's Dream of Jeláleddín renewing the first notes of his immortal song, and chanting again the Hymn of Eternal Life, solemn yet joyous, mystic yet clear: stirring what is deepest in our heart and driving away our sorrow, till 'all the pulses of our being, re-animated, beat anew!'

> *'O ye hopes, that stir within me,*
> *Health comes with you from above!*
> *God is with me, God is in me!*
> *I cannot die, if Life be Love.'*

Thus does our own deep, mystic Singer, Coleridge, echo, in kindred strains, the deepest Faith of Jeláleddín.

William HASTIE

---

1. Werke, x. 468.
2. Specimen Poeseos Persicae. Vienna, 1771.
3. A specimen of Persian Poetry, or Odes of Hafez: with an English Translation and Paraphrase ... chiefly from Baron

Revizky. By John Richardson, F.S.A., 1774. 2nd Ed. by Rousseau, 1802.
4. Grammatik, Poetik und Rhetorik der Perser. Nach dem siebenten Bande des Heft Kolzum, Dargestellt von Friedrich Rückert. Neu herausgegeben von W. Pertsch, 1874, p. 57.
5. A History of Ottoman Poetry, 1900, p. 80. See also Mr. Gibb's Ottoman Poems, 1882, p. xxxvi. Both contain excellent Gazels.
6. Hafiz of Shiraz: Selections from his Poems by H. Bicknell. 1875.
7. E. G. Browne, *Op. cit.* p. 399.
8. If anyone is inclined to think anything in this criticism—which has been much curtailed—too severe, let him or her turn to Von Hammer's Account of Omar Khayyám in Note C and following Remarks.

FIFTY GAZELS OF JELÁLEDDÍN

DONE INTO ENGLISH

'Why heed the Critics who delight to dart
Their sneer-tipped arrows at translator's art?
The poet's work remains his own at last
Though it in other languages be cast.
And in the sky of Fame it still will shine,
By that which made it at the first divine.
But in this foreign dress some soul may see
A hint of that which fascinated me;
Some deep impression be still deeper made
When by our muse-beloved tongue conveyed;
Some beauty be with newer beauty set;
Some thought that will with fresh emotion fret
Some gentle breast, or with strange music sweep
O'er heaving waters of the spirit's deep.'

— ED. ROBESON TAYLOR

I. LIGHT

Until the glorious Sun hath vanquished Night,
The Birds of Day cower trembling with affright.
But lo! a bright glance bids the Tulip ope;
O Heart, awake thou too, in Duty's might.
The Sun's Sword sheds in reddening flush of Dawn
The Blood of Night, and puts the Foe to flight.
The Soul still full of sleep, dreams Night prevails;
But no! Day comes, and triumphs full in sight.
While grey Dawn lingers, dubious yet is Day;
But in Day's glow, who still can doubt the Light.

The Light grows in the East; I in the West

On Mountain top, reflect the Morn's delight.

To Beauty's Sun, I'm but the pale moon here;

Then look from me towards the Sun's face bright.

The Light in East is called Jeláleddín[1];

And here my verse reflects its glowing White.

---

1. The Splendour of the Faith.

II. DEATH AND LIFE

Death endeth sure Life's need and pain;
   Yet Life in fear would Death restrain.
Life only sees dark Death's dread Hand,
Not that bright Cup it offered plain.
So shrinks from Love the tender Heart,
As if from threat of being slain.
But when true Love awakens, dies
The Self, that despot dark and vain.
Then let him die in Night's black hour,
And freely breathe in Dawn again.

III. INVOCATION

Soul of mine, thou dawning Light: Be not far, O be not far!

Love of mine, thou Vision bright: Be not far, O be not far!

Life is where thou smilest sweetly; Death is in thy parting look;

Here mid Death and Life's fierce fight: Be not far, O be not far!

I am East when thou art rising; I am West when thou dost set;

Bring Heaven's own radiant hues to sight: Be not far, O be not far!

See how well my Turban fitteth, yet the Parsee Girdle binds me;

Cord and Wallet I bear light: Be not far, O be not far!

True Parsee and true Brahman, a Christian, yet a Mussulman;

Thee I trust, Supreme by Right: Be not far, O be not far!

In all Mosques, Pagodas, Churches, I do find One Shrine alone;

Thy Face is there my sole delight: Be not far, O be not far!

Thine the World's all-loving Heart; and for it I yearn and pray;

O take not from my Heart thy flight: Be not far, O be not far!

Thee, the World's Eternal Centre, here I circle round in prayer;

Thy absence is last judgment quite: Be not far, O be not far!

Thine, Judgment Day and Blessedness: Mine is Bliss when Thou art nigh;

Keep me circling in thy Might: Be not far, O be not far!

Fair World Rose, O blossom forth; sweet Heart-buds unfold in Love;

Put on the longing Soul's pure White: Be not far, O be not far!

O Rose, hear through Night's silence, how he thrills—thy Nightingale;

As if I did his Notes indite: Be not far, O be not far!

Jeláleddín, all loving, let Love's Heart resist no more:

Hear him chaunting, Day and Night: Be not far, O be not far!

IV. FAITH

All Unbelief is Midnight, but Faith the Night-Lamp's glow;

Then see that no Thief cometh to steal thy Lamp when low.

Our Hope is for the Sunlight, from which the Lamp did shine;

The Light from which it kindled, still feeds its flame below.

But when the Sun hath risen, both Night and Lamp go out;

And Unbelief and Faith then, the higher Vision know.

O Night! Why art thou dreaming? O Lamp! Why flickerest so?

The swift Sun-horses panting, from East their fire-foam throw.

'Tis Night still in the shadow; the village Lamp burns dim;

But in Dawn's Splendour towering, the Peaks Heaven's Glory show.

V. DAWN

The Day has dawned, thy festal Day, O Rose;

Our cheeks all glow in thy bright Ray, O Rose.

Love was the Gardener of the Rose-bed there;

And now thy Flower blooms forth all gay, O Rose.

When Herald Breezes blew: *The Rose!* the Flowers

Kneeling to thee glad Homage pay, O Rose.

The Tulips danced; the Lilies, drinking there,

Their brightest hues to thee display, O Rose.

The Cypress whispered to the Ivy: Wake!

Why dream'st thou, Child? She dreamed thy Play, O Rose;

The Nightingale a thousand long nights through
But trilled thy own sweet Melody, O Rose.
The Heavens more fair assume thy radiant form,
But thou outviest their Phantasy, O Rose.
The Rose a message brings from Paradise
Where Souls for thee all eager stay, O Rose.
The Rose brings greeting to the Soul from Home;
The Soul forgets thee not for aye, O Rose.
The Rose unfolds the Sign of Beauty there:
God's Seal Himself the Poets say, O Rose.
The Soul crowns all Man's festal Cup of Joy;
That he with thee may breathe Life's May, O Rose.
The Rose is twined in all Life's gladdest Bonds,
That Love from Man ne'er flee away, O Rose.
Be closed in Buds thy Lips; but there let shine
The Smile that ever in thee lay, O Rose.

VI. ALLAH HU!

Sound Drum and mellow Flute, resounding: Allah hu[1]!

Dance, ruddy Dawn, in Gladness bounding: Allah hu!

Sun exalted in the Centre, O thou streaming Light;

Soul of all wheeling Planets rounding: Allah hu!

O Hearts! O Worlds! how soon your Dancing all would stop,

Did not His Power sustain astounding! Allah hu!

Love mazy, winding, changing, all embraces,

The Night, the Dawn, the Day, resounding: Allah hu!

Boom, Sea! on Shore, and Rock, thy Music praising God;

O Nightingale to Rose trill, sounding: Allah hu!

O Soul, what if one Star should falter in the Dance?

His Will is Order ever founding: Allah hu!

Who knows Love's mazy circling, ever lives in God;

For Death, he knows, is Love abounding: Allah hu!

---

1. He is God.

VII. SPRING

O Eyes, go forth the Spring to view,
That smiles upon our Plains anew.
A Heavenly Child in cradling Flowers,
Sweet Breath from Skies unclouded drew.
The Morning Breeze his Nurse, that rocked
His Cradle, with soft Lullings due.
The Baby feigns to sleep, and blinks,
Shutting his little Eyelids two.
And when the Lids are oped again,
The Eyebrows drip with sparkling Dew.
The Bees hum round and busy sip

The Nectar, and make Honey new.

O come, and let the Baby's smiles

And Laughter, pierce thee through and through.

O come, and leave your wintry Cell,

And let Heaven's Light thy Life renew.

And build new Cells with honey'd Wax,

Plann'd like the Bees' six-sided, true.

And warmed by radiant Fire of Flowers,

Old Winter's reign of Death undo.

Regret is dead; Love lives again;

New Life transforms the Landscape's Hue.

Bold enter, then, green Spring's loved Haunts,

And drink fresh Wine, nor fear to rue.

And drinking full Love's sweetest Draught,

The glowing Heart new Love shall woo.

Love wakes afresh in Earth and Heaven;

The Rose in green, the Sun in blue.

O Nightingale, behold thy Rose!

O Eagle, thy bright Sun pursue!

VIII. SPRING'S FESTIVAL

Our Fasting is over; 'tis Spring's festal Day: Hallelu!

O dearest Guest welcome, all Sorrow's away: Hallelu!

O Love once forsaken, forsaken Heart now be forsaken;

Thy loved One has come, and for ever will stay: Hallelu!

The Parting is parted; the Sev'rance at last is all sever'd;

The Union united, without more delay: Hallelu!

The Flight is now flown off; the Banishment's pain is now banished;

All distant the Distance; our Bird Nest all gay: Hallelu!

The Moon in the Heavens, the Rose in the Heart, in Love's Garden;

The King in his Palace, proud Banners display: Hallelu!

Life stirs in the Rootlet; soft Sap in the Leaflet is spreading;

Green Buds on the Branches are crowning his Sway: Hallelu!

Let come our Foe hated, for now will he meet our Defender;

We scorn and defy him, all safe now for aye: Hallelu!

Yea, flood me all over, all over with Fire of Love burning;

Now well can I bear it; I'll ne'er burn away: Hallelu!

And now it is certain my Soul is bound up in Salvation;

And all of Earth's sadness is sunk in Earth's clay: Hallelu!

O Chalice full brimming, poured out for the thirst of the worlds;

We thank thee, we bless thee, and drink while we pray: Hallelu!

Long parch'd lay the World, a Desert profane, till thy Breath came

On Wings of the Morning, when bright the Dew lay: Hallelu!

We longed as we waited for Spring's Sun our Life to renew;

Jeláleddín's warm Breath from East came to-day: Hallelu!

IX. DEPENDENCE

I am the Vine; Strong Elm, O give me leave,
All round thee my fond Tendrils now to weave.
I am the Ivy; be my Cedar Trunk,
That I no more to Earth's damp soil may cleave.
I am the Bird; O come, be my light Wings,
That soaring I yon azure Heaven retrieve.
I am the Steed; O come and be my spur,
That quick the Victor Goal may me receive.
I am the Rosebud; O be my own Rose,
That gaudy Earth-weeds ne'er my Heart deceive.
I am the East; then rise in me, O Sun,

Flame up in Light, and all my Pain relieve.

I am the Night; O be my Starry Crown,

That in Life's darkness I nor fear, nor grieve.

X. MYSTICAL UNION

With Thy sweet Soul, this Soul of mine—
Hath mixed as Water doth with Wine.
Who can the Wine and Water part,
Or me and Thee when we combine?
Thou art become my greater Self;
Small Bounds no more can me confine.
Thou hast my Being taken on,
And shall not I now take on Thine?
Me Thou for ever hast affirmed,
That I may ever know Thee mine.
Thy Love has pierced me through and through,

Its Thrill with Bone and Nerve entwine.

I rest a Flute laid on Thy Lips;

A Lute I on Thy Breast recline.

Breathe deep in me that I may sigh;

Yet strike my Strings, and Tears shall shine.

So sweet my Tears, my Sighs so sweet,

I to the World its Joys resign.

Thou restest in my inmost Soul

Whose depths the mirror'd Heaven define.

O Pearl in my Mussel Shell:

O Diamond in my darkest Mine!

My Honey is in Thee dissolved;

O Milk of Life, so mild, so fine!

Our Sweetnesses all blent in Thee,

Give infant Lips their Smiles benign.

Thou crushest me to Drops of Rose;

Nor 'neath the Press do I repine.

In Thy sweet Pain is Pain forgot;

For I, Thy Rose, had this design.

Thou bad'st me blossom on Thy Robe,

And mad'st me for all eyes Thy Sign.

And when Thou pour'st me on the World,

It blows in Beauty, all Divine.

XI. IDENTITY

Although thy Brightness glistens in the Sun, indeed;

Yet is my Light with thine all radiant, One, indeed!

Thou mad'st of Dust all glitt'ring the circling Heavens above;

Yet will with mine thy Spirit ne'er Union shun, indeed!

To Dust return the Heavens; again Heavens spring from Dust;

Yet hast thou in my Being thy own Life spun, indeed!

Now have the Words Eternal that through Heaven's vastness ring,

Found Home in human Bosom, and dearer none, indeed!

Thou hast the Sunbeams hidden, that in the Diamond glow,

Deep, deep in Earth's dark Chambers, a Wonder done, indeed!

See, though in vile Soil feeding, and drinking filthy slime,

To yon Rose peerless Beauty, in Love, hath run, indeed!

O Heart, and be it thou swimmest in Flood, or glow'st in Fire,

The same are Fire and Flood: Be pure, my Son, indeed!

O Mevlana, at Morning I woke, and found with thee,

My Eyes from Tears all brighten'd, and Heaven now won, indeed!

XII. CONFESSION

O Love, to thee I own, I wept in Night's dark Thought;

But now thy radiant Sun to me hath bright Day brought.

O Soul of my own Soul, my I as I am Thou:

Thou art the All, and I in thee have all I sought.

Thou art Life's Sweetness self, Intoxication full,—

The brimming Sea of Pearls, the Gold to pureness wrought.

Whoe'er approaches thee, must first his Soul resign;

He dies beneath thy frown, lives when thy Smile is caught.

Thy Favour thrills in fear the trembling Lover's heart,

Till comes thy Wrath and smites his Weakness into Naught.

XIII. DISCORDIA CONCORS

I saw how Sunward soaring, an Eagle cleaved the air;

And how in Shadow sitting, there coo'd a Turtle pair.

I saw how o'er the Heavens, the Clouds in Herds rush'd wild;

And how close round the Shepherd the Lambkins gather'd fair.

I heard the Stars all asking: When shall we rise again?

And Buds in Seedlings folded sigh: Doth Love for us care?

I saw a Grass blade blossom at Morn and fade at Night;

While Cedars braved a thousand Years the Tempests raging there.

I saw old Ocean's Billows like Kings all crowned with foam,

Then flung from Rocks, down fallen, like Penitents in Prayer.

I saw a Dewdrop sparkling, nor did it Danger dread;

But, soon consumed, it vanish'd, that sun-bright Jewel rare.

I saw close crowding Mankind new Towns and Castles rear;

And swarming Ants heaped Hillocks up, with Winter's garner'd fare.

I saw the Warhorse prancing and trampling golden Grain;

And all his Hoofs were redden'd with the Blood of Love's Despair.

I saw the Winter weaving from Flakes a Robe of Death;

And the Spring found Earth in Mourning, all naked, lone and bare.

I heard Time's Loom a-whirring that wove the Sun's dim Veil;

I saw a Worm a-weaving in Life-threads its own Lair.

I saw the Great was Smallest, and saw the Smallest Great;

For God had set His Likeness on all the Things that were.

XIV. RENOVATION

Come, O Springtide of my Love: the World, again, make New!

Light in Heaven and Flowers on Earth, o'er Hill and Plain, make New!

With the blue gleaming Sun-gem, set thy new green Turban on;

And o'er the Fields all verdant, thy floral Train, make New!

Paint Meadows fresh with bright Buds, let Hedgerows sprout once more;

Rose Breast-Knots, slender Lilies in bathing Rain, make New!

Melt with thy warm Breath Winter's iced Coat and frozen Spear;

With tender Smile shame Hatred; Peace, ending Pain, make New!

The Air pines for thy Whisper, and the Rose's Breath is faint;

Then from Slumber rouse thy Zephyrs, and the feather'd Vane, make New!

Roll, Thunder, pour thy Bounty adown from bursting Cloud;

Now bathe from Head to Foot free, and Death's Disdain, make New!

Strike, Pine, upon the Wind-drum! O Plane-tree, clap thy Hands!

Brooding Love, the dreamy birth Down on feather'd Train, make New!

Vines, twine around the Elm Trees, God's Glory showing fair;

While Violets kiss the soft Sod, Spring's sweet Hymn-strain, make New!

Hyacinths the Tulips fondle; woos Rose the Nightingale.

While Turtles coo in low Notes, my Song's Refrain, make New!

Kindle Altar-fire in Blossoms, in Fragrance Incense burn;

The Pan Pipes that in dead Grass, long have silent lain, make New!

Let Leaves shoot quivering Tongues out, Love's Questionings in Play;

And whisp'ring to each other, Love's Wrangling vain, make New.

Hark! How the Morning Breezes, at rosy Dawn all call:

Up! Up! O Friend, 'tis Spring-time: the Soul's glad Reign, make New!

Behold the Spring in Glory! O thou Alchemist of Flowers,

Smelt the fiery Glow to Blossoms; our World, again, make New!

XV. REVOLVING IN MYSTIC DANCE

Come! Come! Thou art the Soul, the Soul so dear, Revolving!

Come! Come! Thou art the Cedar, the Cedar's Spear, Revolving!

O Come! The Well of Light up-bubbling springs;

And Morning Stars exult, in Gladness sheer, Revolving!

Of the o'er-arching Heavens, the Highest is the Seventh;

But over all thou stretchest, bright, and clear, Revolving!

In warmest Arms of Love thou hold'st me clasped,

And thee I hold enclasped, soft breathing, near, Revolving!

In Sunbeams dance the Motes, by Sunlight grasped,

O Sunlight, grasping me, dispel my Fear, Revolving!

The Motes dance mute, yet telling all of Love;

O silent Love! Teach me thy own Dance here, Revolving!

XVI. THE SOUL IN ALL

A mote I in the Sunshine, yet am the Sun's vast Ball;

I bid the Sun spread Sunlight, and make the Mote be small.

I am the Morning Splendour; I am the Evening Breeze;

I am the Leaf's soft Rustle; the Billow's Rise and Fall.

I am the Mast and Rudder, the Steersman and the Ship;

I am the Cliff out-jutting, the Reef of Coral Wall.

I am the Bird Ensnarer, the Bird and Net as well;

I am both Glass and Image; the Echo and the Call.

JELÁLEDDÍN RÚMÍ

I am the Tree and Branches, and all the Birds thereon;

I am both Thought and Silence, Tongues' Speech, and Ocean Squall.

I am the Flute when piping, and Man's Soul breathing breath;

I am the sparkling Diamond, and Metals that enthrall.

I am the Grape enclustered, the Wine-press and the Must;

I am the Wine, Cup-bearer, and crystal Goblet tall.

I am the Flame and Butterfly, which round it circling flits;

I am the Rose and Nightingale, the Rose's Passioned Thrall.

I am the Cure and Doctor, Disease and Antidote;

I am the Sweet and Bitter, the Honey and the Gall.

I am the War and Warrior, the Victor and the Field;

I am the City peaceful, the Battle and the Brawl.

I am the Brick and Mortar, the Builder and the Plan,

I am the Base and Gable, new House and ruined Hall.

I am the Stag and Lion, the Lamb and black-maw'd Wolf;

I am the Keeper of them, who shuts them in one Stall.

I am the Chain of Beings, the Ring of circling Worlds;

The Stages of Creation, where'er it rise or fall.

I am what is and is not; I am—O Thou who know'st,

Jeláleddín, O tell it—I AM the Soul in All!

XVII. RESPONSIBILITY

O thou who hast come safely, into this Being's Land;

Strange, thou thyself not knowest, how thou didst reach its Strand.—

Straight from the great Shah's Chamber, thou cam'st to Being's Town,

Sent here to do the Business which he himself had planned.

The Lord gave, then, to prove thee, Capacity to do;

And as entrusted Capital, thy Sum of Life in hand.

How has the Market's Turmoil confused thy Sense and Brain;

THE FESTIVAL OF SPRING FROM THE DÍVÁN ... | 99

That thou the Pledge entrusted, can yet not understand?

O cease to dream and rouse thee; and do thy Duty well;

Buy choicest Pearls more wisely, and give not Gold for Sand.

When thou to Home returnest, thou'lt see Him sitting there;

Thy Lord with His Book open, and His own faithful Band.

He will hold count, and reckon all that Himself did give;

And ask how thou did'st use it, when under His Command.

And then will come His Blessing, or Curse, both just and sure,

According as thy Credit, or thy Debt, summed up shall stand.

XVIII. ACTION

Awake! 'Tis Day! Rise up, O Youthful Mussulman!

Pack quick thy Goods and Baggage, and catch the Caravan.

O List! I hear it coming, 'twill sweep past while you sleep;

Hark! Tinkling Bells are calling to come, while come you can.

When once the Desert Sand-storm has o'er the Foot-prints blown,

You them will find no longer, however close you scan.

Up! Brace yourself for Action, as a Man all prompt and bold;

And waste not Life fond, dreaming, in idlesse, pining, wan.

Think of your noble Forbears, the gallant Youth of old;

Of Rustum, bravest Hero; of Sal, the Pehlevan.[1]

Be, too, of Right the Champion, Knight of the spotless Sun!

Fall not a Prey to Darkness, o'erthrown by Ahriman.

When once in struggle valiant, the earthly Soul is slain,

The Heavenly Soul bears proudly Life's Banner in the Van.

When thou thyself hast conquered, and triumphed in the Fight;

A diamond Ring thou'lt ever shine, in our Lord Shah's Divan.

---

1. Pehlevan, *i.e.* of the old heroic Age. 'Rustum, the "Hercules" of Persia, and Zál his Father, whose exploits are among the most celebrated in the Sháhnáma' (Fitzgerald). Compare Matthew Arnold's 'Sohrab and Rustum. An Episode.'

XIX. BONDAGE

Complain not that in Chains, thou here art firmly bound;

Complain not that Earth's Yoke, doth crush thee to the Ground.

Complain not that the World is but a Prison wide;

'Tis only thy complainings that build thy Dungeon round.

And ask not how Life's Riddle will finally unfold;

For soon without thy asking, unfolded 'twill be found.

Say not Love has forsaken or yet forgotten thee;

Love ne'er has Man forsaken; thy Words all falsely sound.

Nor tremble when Death dreaded appears in Terror's Form;

He falls before the Hero, who is with Courage crowned.

Ne'er chase the Phantom, Pleasure; for like a hungry Lion,

'Twill turn and rend in pieces the Hunter most renowned.

Throw not thyself in Fetters; else will Men sternly say:

Complain not of thy Fetters; for thou thyself hast bound.

XX. LOVE'S FREEDOM

O Bird, that freest to Freedom win;
Love caged thee in that Prison thin.
O Soul, if thou, too, wouldst be free,
Then love the Love that shuts thee in.
'Tis Love that twisteth every Snare;
'Tis Love that snaps the Bond of Sin.
Love sounds the Music of the Spheres;
Love echoes through Earth's harshest Din.
Love fills with Fragrance Heaven's sweet Air;
Love's deft Hands Life's gold Fibres spin.
The World is God's pure Mirror clear,

To Eyes when free from Clouds within.

With Love's own Eyes the Mirror view,

And there see God to Self akin.

Then praise Him, Soul, enflamed with Love

As Larks in Dawn, new Songs begin.

XXI. IN MY HEART

O, what a Throb of Toil is in my Heart!
What Shrine's crowd-trodden Soil is in my Heart!

The Spring has come; again the Sower sows,

And all the Season's Moil is in my Heart.

The Veil which hid the World's fair face is drawn;

Disclosed, its inmost Coil is in my Heart.

The Heart must higher rise, than setting Suns;

The Sun-dance nought can foil is in my Heart.

The Heart has well been named the Shah's own throne;

And warm anointing Oil is in my Heart.

The Heart's deep Ocean rolls a thousand waves;

And rich Pearl-diver's Spoil is in my Heart.

Jeláleddín! The Heart is sure both Mine and Mint;

For Fire, as Gold did boil, is in my Heart.

XXII. NOT DEAF TO LOVE

O Brother hear! Be deaf no more, to Love:
Thy heart now open to its Core, to Love!
Hast thou in Pride, all vain, upraised thy Head?
Come bend it now down to the Floor, to Love.
In Dust thou shalt new living Grace receive,
As Spring awakes the Landscape frore, to Love.
And once thou hast put on Love's Leaves and Flowers,
Comes golden Fruit in Autumn hoar, to Love.
And when thou fadest sere, then burn thyself;
And give thy Ashes, all Earth bore, to Love.

And wing'd, from Ashes wilt thou fairer rise;

And with Love's highest Message soar, to Love.

XXIII. ASSIMILATION

New Sword from Maker's Hand, in Edge and Point all bright;

See that in dirty Scabbard, it rust not, out of Sight!

Gold that in Miser's Coffer, in Blackness meanly lay,

Upon the Shah's Throne gleaming, becomes a World's Delight.

When full Clouds pour the Rain-drops, lo! every glad Tree drinks;

Fruits redden on the Apple tree, as Leaves grow pale in Fright.

This Stalk an empty Pipe still, in that sweet Sugar swells;

Yet both did sip the same Tank, at Morning, Noon, and Night.

One Deer distils perfumed Musk, another bitterest Gall,

Yet grazed together, side by side, upon the self-same Height.

Two creeping Worms together fed upon the same green Leaf;

One spins mere useless Theadlets, the other Silk aright.

The Bee's Lip, and the Snake's sucked from the self-same Flower;

The one made Honey's Sweetness, the other Poison's Bite.

One dines, and all his Nutriment transmutes to Life divine;

Another's Food is souring to Hatred and to Spite.

One's Eyes drink Light till blinded; the other stores it up,

And glows in rosy Brightness, Love-robed in red and white.

Be pure in all thy Members, and from Nature's golden Tree

Pluck God's own Blessing daily, and grow in Manhood's Might.

XXIV. CLEANLINESS

Clean be kept thy Garment, and
   Clean be kept thy Mouth and Hand.
Clean thy Garment from false Gawds
Clean from all Earth's Filth thy Hand.
Clean thy Heart from earthly Spite;
Clean thy Lips from Greed's Demand.
Outer Threshhold ever clean,
Clean within let all Things stand.
House all clean, might entertain
Angel from the Heavenly Land.
Clean the Food, and clean the cup,

Clean the Wall from smoking Brand.

Son! Thy outward Cleanliness

Pledge of inward is, when scanned.

Clean let Hand and Mouth be kept;

Clean thy Garment's every Strand.

XXV. WHERE IS HE?

I ask all I meet: Where is He?
In me incomplete: Where is He?
The Tree of my Thought stretch'd on high,
Reach'd not to His Seat: Where is He?
I ask of the Wanderers by Day:
My loved One, most sweet, Where is He?
I ask of the Keepers of Vines:
My loved One, most sweet, Where is He?
I rush through the Woods and the Fields,
And ask the Stag fleet: Where is He?
At Night when in Darkness He hides,

In Fear I repeat: Where is He?

I ask of the Sun and the Moon,

And Stars in retreat: Where is He?

He is not with me. Who has seen

The Path of His Feet? Where is He?

O Master, if thou hast Him found,

O tell, I entreat: Where is He?

XXVI. LOVE'S SLAVERY

Come, and be Love's willing Slave;
 Thee Love's Slavery will save.
Leave the Slavery of the World,
Take Love's Service, sweet and brave.
The Free, the World makes enslaved;
Aye to Slaves, Love Freedom gave.
As the Bird freed from the Egg,
From the World release I crave.
Free me from the Shell that clings;
Give me Life as from the Grave.
O Love, the Quail in Spring's Free Fields,

In Songs of wildest Joy must rave.

XXVII. PSYCHE IN TEARS

Psyche sits, and lovelier seems;
    Ah! she of her Lover dreams!
Still his Kiss she softly feels;
Still his Smile in Fancy gleams.
But in Light she fain would see
Love's own Self, nor wrong it deems.
Trembling her white Hand hath ta'en
Lamp to light, as Fancy schemes.
There by flickering Flame she scans
Beauty which she Heaven esteems.
But the fluttering Oil did shake,

Shamed to find eclipsed its Beams.

Fell one hot Drop on Love's Hand:

Oh! the Lover waken'd screams!

Love light-pinion'd flies away;

Psyche's Wings, Tears drench in Streams.

XXVIII. SUBSTITUTIONAL

Where the cleansing Water fails,
    Sand, as Substitute, avails.
This, at Need, the Prophet gave;
And his Rule to-day prevails.
Know ye, O Believers, why?
Hear the Truth the Sage unveils.—
The Desert oft no Water shows,
But never Sand the Traveller fails.
From the Desert I will guide
Him who me as Leader hails.
To where living Waters flow,

To the Garden Love empales.

Bathe there in Abundance full,

Where no hostile Drought assails.

Full, that Stream Bath, now enjoy'd,

Freedom from Sand Bath entails.

So from Formulas made free,

Spirit Life o'er all prevails.—

Master! Thy high Soul hath seen

Truth through all its hiding Veils.

XXIX. GOD'S THRONE

Unto your Fathers, Allah did make known
This which they handed down and made your own,—
That all who pray My Face may clearly see,
I sit exalted high on Heaven's great Throne.
As I in Heaven, so you I place on Earth,
That I in my Vicegerents, may be shown.
Serve Me then, that the World may serve you too
Made to do good—this is your End alone.
The World was fitly made to help you well:
No Traitors be; let all my Justice own.

And glorify the Maker of the World,

Until the Rose of Peace hath round you blown.

XXX. THE LION OF GOD

Fairest Flower beneath the Skies:
   Ali Abutaleb's Son!
Fairest Flower in Paradise:
Ali Abutaleb's Son!
God's brave Lion, lamb-like, gentle,
Clearest Mirror, ever bright:
Pure in Faith, without Disguise:
Ali Abutaleb's Son!
Next the Prophet is thy Place,
All his Splendour flashing round:
Thy bright Light too floods our Eyes:

Ali Abutaleb's Son!

By Renouncing, daring Soul,

And by braving Danger too:

Thou hast won the Hero's Prize:

Ali Abutaleb's Son!

Straight thy Strength of Soul and Limb

Bore thee to the thickest Fight:

Death thy giant Thews despise:

Ali Abutaleb's Son!

All the Paths we tread to-day,

Thou hast traced them, Son of Light!

Let on us thy Beams arise:

Ali Abutaleb's Son!

Leader, Guide, and Champion true,

Ever foremost in the Ván:

Where thou leadest, Honour lies:

Ali Abutaleb's Son!

Maulānā, in Hymn of Praise

Thee I laud, Jeláleddín!

Even as thou praisest wise,

Ali Abutaleb's Son!

XXXI. SELF-REALISATION

When I knew myself a Thorn, soft Rosebuds' Swell

I sought for then;

When I saw myself all bitter, sweet Honey's Cell

I sought for then.

When I saw myself all Poison, I quaffed Life's Stream

as Antidote;

When I saw myself Lees turbid, Wine's clear Foam Bell

I sought for then.

When I saw myself all sour Fruit, I caught the ripening

Sunbeams' Glow;

When I saw myself droop feebly, the breezy Fell

I sought for then.

When I saw myself all blinded, the healing Power of Jesus' Hand;

When I knew it could the Darkness from my Eyes dispel

I sought for then.[1]

Love's Touch became my Eyesalve, and all my Soul's

dull Blindness fled;

And, my Heart of Thirst a-dying, His sweet, pure Well

I sought for then.

I am Fire that never burneth; and thou, the Wind

that makes it burn;

O thou Wind, with my Fire playing, aye in me dwell:

I sought for then.

---

1. Rückert avoids the name of Jesus; not so Von Hammer.

XXXII. THY HAND!

Lord, that I thee may find, O stretch to me thy Hand!

Close-clasped for ever, kind, O stretch to me thy hand!

O'er Earth it gathers dark, and ever deeper here

Where dim cross Footpaths wind, O stretch to me thy Hand!

The Malice of the World and deadly Hate I know;

Where the Danger grows defined, O stretch to me thy Hand!

The Pilgrim's Journey still is threatened by the Foe;

But to thwart the Ill designed, O stretch to me thy Hand!

O come, and let it press upon this burning Heart;

Though Tears my glad Eyes blind, O stretch to me thy Hand!

Fair Moon, up to thy Palace all shining, I would climb;

But lest I halt behind, O stretch to me thy hand!

XXXIII. THE PRIESTS

Love called to Men from Heaven's bright Gate,

'Who look to God now, soon and late?'

''Tis we who look aloft to God,'

To Love replied the Priests elate.

Love cried 'How can ye look on high,

Who thus your Forms and Words inflate?

Ye cannot see where pure Light dwells,

So full your Eyes of Greed and Hate.

Your dark Deeds dim the Noontide's Ray;

Ye shame the Sun while thus ye prate.

The Grace that sits enthroned on high,

Can ne'er its Claim of Faith abate.

Nor can the Just One justly give

The Hearing which ye supplicate.

O ere ye look to Heaven again,

Put off all earthly Pride and State.

Your Hearts let Love, not Hatred, rule;

Then look to God, and on Him wait!'

XXXIV. THE PILGRIMS

The Pilgrims hail the Kaaba's sacred Ground,
When they at last the holy Fane have found.
They see a House of Stone, sublime, revered,
All girt by steep and barren Cliffs around.
They march'd in Hope expecting God to see;
For this they toiled, and still their Prayers abound.
But when all fervent they the Threshold tread,
They hear a voice from out the Temple sound:
'Why pray ye thus, O Fools, to Clay and Stone?
Revere the House for which the Pure are bound.

The Heart's own House, Shrine of the True, the One:

O blest are they whose Striving there is crown'd!

Blest those who tread no Desert's weary Way,

But rest at Home in peace, like Shems renown'd.'[1]

---

1. Rosen, whom I have followed in the last two lines, calls this 'an incomparable Gazel.' Shems-ud-Din (The Sun of Religion) was Jeláleddín's celebrated Teacher and revered Master, whose name he introduced into his Gazels instead of his own, whence his Divan became entitled the 'Divan of Shems of Tabriz.' Rückert, however, substitutes Jeláleddín's own name, in accordance with Western usage and fact.

XXXV. MANY FAITHS, ONE LORD

Our House has many Doors indeed,
But all to One Lord inward lead.
And all who reach this Lord must pray,
With Forehead on the Ground, and plead.
And many in the House born blind,
The Lord's commands yet hear and heed.
The Lame there too can Service give,
They all perform House Tasks at need.
Yea, even the Wind with panting Breath,
Comes in, the Hearth's low Fire to feed.
Each one must do his Part as bid,

No one can choose his Share or Deed.

Yet many deem them free, nor know

The Bond that binds them firm decreed.

But if thou humbly bear thy Bond,

It holds a Crown of Flowers in Seed.

Plight Troth, and Grace will answer Sure,

For Love's Vow seals the highest Creed.

Servant! To Fellow-servants shew

The lowly Mien no Hate will breed.

Forbearing be! Thy Over-Lord

No Pleasure hath in Pride or Greed.

Can one e'er claim to enter bold

Who Entrance never would concede?

Who dares to haggle with the Master,

He drives them from His Doors with Speed.

XXXVI. LOVE ABSOLUTE

Love lies not in Book, or Letter, or well reason'd Tome—O no!

Love lives not in Cell of Penance, nor in gloomy Home—O no!

From the Green of Spring eternal shoots up the Tree of Life;

Yet Milkyway and Pleiad reach not Love's Dome—O no!

Reason dismounts before her, Desire her Charioteer;

So long the Way no slower to Love's Realm would come—O no!

While thou art still a Lover, the Longing in thee moves;

But when thou art the Loved One, thou need'st not roam—O no!

Wrecked Landsmen shriek in Terror, though saving spars float round;

The Pilot steeped in rapture, recks not Death's Foam—O no!

Jeláleddín, thy soul in Ocean melts in joy:

Thyself all Consecration, no Novice far from Home—O no!

XXXVII. RENUNCIATION

Since he to me his loving Heart has shown,
I give my Life to him, as All his own.
The Body's House becomes his Temple now,
Until the Soul herself to Heav'n hath flown.
The Earthly Life is Offering far too small;
Then let the Eternal, silent All atone.
Jeláleddín in self-negation found
The Rose of Life divinely fair, full blown.

XXXVIII. ALL FULNESS

Ever shall I more desire
    Than Time's bounded Needs require.
Ever as more Flowers I pluck,
Blossoms new gay Spring attire.
And when through the Heavens I sweep,
Rolling Spheres will flash new Fire.
Perfect Beauty only can
True Eternal Love inspire.

XXXIX. FRIENDSHIP

The Rose is aye Love's dearest, sweetest Sign;

To my Friend's Heart, I give this Rose of mine.

Clear Thought dies out in Love's absorbed Delight,

As Weeds grow pale before the Rose and pine.

The Rose hides in her Heart the piercing Thorn,

For deepest hidden Pains with Love entwine.

The Rose is Beauty perfected in One,

Her Charms all glowing, Heaven and Earth outshine.

The full blown Rose in Splendour dims the Sun;

Each quivering Leaflet shows a Moon's design.

The Sun's sphered Light is moulded in her Form,

While bright-eyed Stars keep watch around her Shrine.

O Sun, the Rose that made the Moon to grow,

To my Heart's Friend give Love and Joy divine!

XL. THE FRIEND SUPREME

O what a Friend is mine!
 O what a burning Flame!
My Heart was parched and dead,
Till His Breath o'er me came.
When I before Him fled,
By Love's Keen Pang distressed;
He cried, Why dost thou flee?
Thou art thyself to blame.
At Night I asked the Moon,
Where hid my Moon still stayed?
She said, My Cheek grew pale,

In Fear when told His Name.

The Sun, when risen, I asked,

And why art thou so dim?

He said, My Eyelids dull

In Tears have veil'd their Shame.

And to the Sea I said,

Why canst thou not be still?

She answer'd, Deep Unrest

Will leave me ne'er the Same.

I cried to Fire, Flame Queen:

Why flickerest thou So?

On me, she cried, He looked,

And quench'd all Earthly Aim.

I shouted then, O Wind:

Why hurriest to and fro?

She gasped, His Breath consumes me,

Whene'er my Pace I tame!

But what in me, too, meaneth

This elemental Strife?

The Cup in my Hand shaketh,

And Fever thrills my Frame.
In Revel's Glow enraptured,
His Love I know my own:
Then, come, pour foaming Wine out,
Till o'er All flows His Name.

XLI. IMMORTALITY

I am the Bird of Paradise;
   And still my Nest is in the Skies.
I am the Spirit Falcon, flown
From Heav'n's Tent, where it open lies.
But in my eager Chase of Prey,
I fell to where new Sense Worlds rise.
I am the Hero of Mount Kaf,[1]
Who braves the Death the Weakling flies.
I look on high, until he call
Me home from this far Enterprise.
I look up steadfast, searching keen,

Until my Gaze the Throne descries.

There all secure my Nest bides near

The Tree of Life, where Nothing dies.

---

1. Simurg. Also the name of the Phoenix (Von Hammer), but according to Steingass, the Griffin.

XLII. THE FIRST AND LAST

Thou art of all Man's Joys the Spring;
Life's honey'd Sweetness thou dost bring.
My gather'd Pearls, from Bosom full,
Before thy Feet my glad Hands fling.
The Souls love-moved, are circling on,
Like Streams to their great Ocean King.
Thou art the Sun of all Men's Thoughts;
Thy Kisses are the Flowers of Spring.
The Dawn is pale from yearning Love;
The Moon in Tears is sorrowing.
Thou art the Rose; and deep for thee,

In Sighs, the Nightingales still sing.

O can my Love me so despise,

That he my Heart with Pain can wring?

O Wine of Life, all fragrant, pour,

And soothe the Pain of Death's last Sting!

XLIII. MYSTIC LOVE DANCE

On with the Dance! We fly upon the Wings of Love;

We glow in all the Joys and scorn the Stings of Love.

I heard Love joyous calling from out the Realm of Death;

Lo! God hath drown'd dark Death now in living Springs of Love.

The Power of Life that loosen'd my Band when I was born,

That Hour my Mother gave me the Leading Strings of Love.

I asked Love's Self, fond nursing: How shall I Love escape?

She said: There is no Outlet from encircling Rings of Love.

Love's magic Mirror radiates a Thousand Worlds most fair;

And wondering Eyes look dazzled on all it brings of Love.

Thy Body's gold surrender to Love's refining Flames,

The Gold is Dross till boiling, all pure, it sings of Love.

I tell thee why the Ocean aye tosses glittering Spray:

It dances and it glances with Gems, Playthings of Love.

I tell thee how was Mankind a-formed from Earthy Dust:

God in the Dust inbreathèd sweet Whisperings of Love.

I tell thee why the Heavens for ever circle round:

God's Throne set in the Centre, draws All on Wings of Love.

I tell thee why the Zephyr at Morn so softly blows:

To flutter every Leaflet with the Kiss it flings of Love.

I tell thee why Night hideth in Veil so dark her Face:

She makes the World a bridal Tent, and darkling sings of Love.

I can divine all Riddles Creation puts to me,

For to her Riddles Ever, Man the Answer brings of Love.

XLIV. DREAM FEAR

O Love, the Realm of Dreams
    Is thine; they come, unsought:
With fiery Weapons, throng'd,
As if whole Armies fought.
The Standard of thy Rule,
Hot Hearts bear in the Van;
It flames till Worlds, o'ercome,
Beneath thy Sway are brought.
Thou, ever and again,
Sendst out a Phantom Form;
Till cower weak, trembling Souls,

Like Children terror-wrought.

But when a Soul resigns,

Thou, Victor, marchest in:

A Conqueror—lovelier far

Than ever Soul had thought.

XLV. THE CRY OF LOVE

My Soul sends up to Heaven each Night the Cry of Love!

Hu! Hu![1]

God's starry Beauty draws with Might the Cry of Love!

Hu! Ya!

Bright Sun and Moon each Morn dance in my Heart at Dawn;

And waking me in Daylight, excite the Cry of Love!

On every Meadow glancing, I see God's Sunbeams play;

And all Creation's Wonders incite the Cry of Love!

The Turtledove embowered, awakened by my Call,

Returns to me in coo'd Delight, the Cry of Love!

Gu! Gu!

The Crag on whose bare Forehead thy Light in Glory falls,

Resounds in Echoes clear, aright the Cry of Love!

Men! Hu!

For all the Flowers sweet blowing in timid Silence there,

For deaf Worms, too, I offer God's Rite, the Cry of Love!

The Ocean's speechless Billows sound ever loud thy Praise;

And all in rolling Anthems recite the Cry of Love!

To thee for every Rosebud and every Dewdrop fair,

And every Gem, deep hidden, I plight the Cry of Love!

Hu! Ya!

I, All in All becoming, now clear see God in All;

And up for Union yearning, takes Flight the Cry of Love!

Hu! Hu!

---

1. Rückert does not give these Exclamations, but Von Hammer does. Hu!=He!

XLVI. NIGHT THOUGHT

Sleep not, O Thought, my Guest—the livelong Night!

I bring thee Friendship's best—the livelong Night!

Thou, like an Angel's Breath, from Heaven hast come,

To heal me while I rest—the livelong Night!

Banish dull Slumber, let Heaven's Mystery sing,

From out his secret Nest—the livelong Night!

Shine clear, ye circling Stars, that in your Rays,

The Soul its Vision test—the livelong Night!

Ye Diamonds, sparkling in your dark Retreats,

Rival the starry West—the livelong Night!

Soar up, O Eagle, Sunwards—higher, higher!

Be still thy Flight up pressed—the livelong Night!

Thank God, the World now sleeps; alone are God

And I, all God-possess'd—the livelong Night!

The Night is calm and deep, and Heaven's own Lyre,

Sounds soft, as Star-caress'd—the livelong Night!

War's Turmoil whirling through the starry Streets,

New spheral Choirs attest—the livelong Night!

With Lion, Bull, and Ram, all warlike gleam

Orion's Sword and Crest—the livelong Night!

Scorpion and Dragon seize the Crown, while weeps

The Virgin sore opprest—the livelong Night!

My Tongue sinks dumb with rapture, drunk with Love;

Now, Thought, brood, silent, blest—the livelong Night!

{50}

XLVII. UP OUT OF NIGHT

O for Wings to Heaven to soar—

Up out of Night!

A Heart to Struggle to Light's Shore—

Up out of Night!

Lo! How God's Messengers of Love,

In dancing Dawn:

In Life and Light new Worlds restore,

Up out of Night!

See in the West how Daylight there,

Slow Sinking down:

Looks back, with Love all blushing sore,

Up out of Night!

And now in East where she again,

Doth rise all fair;

Blooms Rose Dawn, brightening as of yore,

Up out of Night!

Time's Memories clear and Life's bright Hopes

Together twine:

Hands loving stretch to us once more,

Up out of Night!

The Eternal Stars all sparkling ope

Their radiant Eyes;

And flash anew deep Wisdom's Lore,

Up out of Night!

And ere Heavens full-blown Rose shall fade,

The endless Day

Shall rise in Bliss at thy Heart's Core,

Up out of Night!

O Nightingale that woos for aye

The Heavenly Rose:

Now, now thy deepest Love Notes pour,

Up out of Night!

XLVIII. ALL ONE

I looked around, and saw in all Heaven's Spaces: One!

In Ocean's rippling Waves and billowy Races: One!

I looked into the Heart, and saw a Sea, wide Worlds

All full of Dreams, and in all Dreaming Faces: One!

Thou art the First, the Last, the Outer, Inner, Whole:

Thy Light breaks through in all Earth's Hues and Graces: One!

Thou seest All from East to furthest Bound of West,

And lo! each Leaf and Flower and Tree Crown traces: One!

Four wild and restive Steeds draw on the World's vast Car;

Thou bridlest them, and rul'st in all their Paces: One!

Air, Fire, Earth, Water melt to One in Fear of thee;

Nor struggle wild, but show in close Embraces: One!

The Hearts of all that live in Earth and Heav'n above,

Beat Praise to thee; nor fails in all their Places—One.

XLIX. O WAKE IN ME

When all the World has gone to rest,
　O Wake in Me!
When tired Eyes close by Sleep opprest,
O Wake in Me!
When Eyes in Heaven all sleepless watch
with Starry gaze,
Make my blind Orbs thy Home as Guest,
O Wake in Me!
When all my outer Gates of Sense,
are shut and bar'd;
Lest, lone, my Soul be fear-possest,

O Wake in Me!

That no grim Power of Darkness through the Gloom around,

My deeper Peace and Calm molest,

O Wake in Me!

From Eden's Garden still soft blown, That fragrant Air

The healing Tree of Life attest,

O Wake in Me!

That once, at least in Dream, Life's Good be here attained,

The Heart no more by pain distrest,

O Wake in Me!

In the moist Midnight dank and drear, where Shadows creep,

Lest Passions vile my Heart infest,

O Wake in Me!

And when Life's Night is gone, and Love's

new dawning Smile

Woos me for ever to thy Breast,

O Wake in Me!

L. JELÁLEDDÍN

Highest Love, where thou art thronèd, here before Thy Throne unseen,

O let me pour my Melodies, my sweetest, highest yet, I ween.

If well-pleasing they ascending reach Thine ear in tones of power,

All their work of soul-subduing comes from Thy own soul serene.

Let them hymn and let them praise thee: let them cry and supplicate:

Where is he to Earth descended, Star from out thy Glory's Sheen?

He his Head with thy soft Roses wreathed, and struck the charmèd String,

Till drunk with Love he passed sweet playing to the Light no cloud can screen.

He beclad in Garments waving here on broken Pillar leaned,

Pouring Songs by which upwafted he hath left this lower Scene.

Hath he now flown to Thy Bosom? Tell me, Love, who here below

Didst his Soul so sweetly cherish, where still cherished hath he been?—

Where the Peoples sink their Banners, where Pride lays her Signs aside,

All their Caste Distinctions blending, where eternal Peace is Queen.

There among the Saints, the purest, of all Zones, is he now found:

Hail! All hail his Memory holy: Maulānā Jelál-ed-Dín!

NOTES.

A. SIR WILLIAM JONES ON THE MYSTICAL POETRY OF THE PERSIANS.

B. HEGEL ON THE CHARACTER OF THE PERSIAN LYRICAL POETRY.

C. VON HAMMER'S ACCOUNT OF OMAR KHAYYÁM.

A. SIR WILLIAM JONES ON THE MYSTICAL POETRY OF THE PERSIANS.

1\. *Epitome of the Mystical System.*—The Persian (and Hindu) mystical Poets 'concur in believing that the souls of men differ infinitely in *degree*, but not at all in *kind*, from the divine Spirit, of which they are particles, and in which they will ultimately be absorbed; that the spirit of God pervades the universe, always immediately present to his work, and consequently always in substance; that he alone is perfect benevolence, perfect truth, perfect beauty; that the love of him alone is real and genuine love, while that of all other objects is absurd and illusory; that the beauties of Nature are faint resemblances, like images in a mirror, of the divine charms; that, from eternity without beginning to eternity without end, the supreme benevolence is occupied in bestowing happiness or the means of attaining it; that men can only attain it by performing their part of the *primal covenant* between them and the Creator; that nothing has a pure absolute existence, but *mind* or *spirit*; that material substances, as the ignorant call them, are no more than gay *pictures* presented continually to our minds by the Sempiternal Artist; that we must beware of attachment to such phantoms, and attach ourselves exclusively to God, who truly exists in us, as we exist solely in him; that we retain, even in this forlorn state of separation from our beloved, *the idea of heavenly beauty*, and *the remembrance of our primeval vows*; that sweet music, gentle breezes, fragrant flowers, perpetually renew the primary *idea*, refresh our fading memory, and melt us with tender affections; that we must cherish those affections, and by abstracting our souls from vanity, that is, from all but God, approximate to his essence, in our final union with which will consist our supreme beatitude. From these principles flow a thousand metaphors and poetical figures, which abound in the sacred poems of the Persians and Hindus.'

2. *The poetical Imagery.*—'Many zealous admirers of Hafiz insist, that by *Wine* he invariably means *devotion*; and they have gone so far as to compose a Dictionary of Words in the *Language*, as they call it, of the Súfis. In that vocabulary *sleep* is explained by *meditation* on the divine perfections, and *perfume* by *hope* of the divine favour; *gales* are *illapses* of grace; *kisses* and *embraces*, the *raptures* of piety; *idolaters, infi-*

dels, and *libertines* are men of the purest *religion*, and their *idol* is the Creator Himself; the *tavern* is a retired Oratory, and its *keeper* a sage instructor; *beauty* denotes the *perfection* of the Supreme Being; *tresses* are the *expansion* of his glory; *lips*, the hidden mysteries of his essence; *down* on the cheek, the world of spirits, who encircle his throne; and a *black mole*, the point of indivisible unity; lastly, *wantonness, mirth*, and *ebriety*, mean religious ardour and abstraction from all terrestrial thoughts.'—Sir William Jones' *Works*, vol. iv. pp. 219, 227.

B. HEGEL ON THE CHARACTER OF THE PERSIAN LYRICAL POETRY.

Continuing the exposition quoted on p. xxi., Hegel goes on to say:—

'In Sublimity proper, the best objects and the most splendid forms are used only as a mere ornament of God, and they serve to proclaim the magnificence and glory of the One, being brought before our eyes only to glorify Him as the Lord of all creatures. But in Pantheism, on the contrary, the Immanence of the Divine in the objects, raises the mundane, natural, and human existence itself, to a more substantial glory of its own. The actual Life of the Spiritual in the phenomena of Nature and in human relationships, animates and spiritualises them in themselves, and establishes in turn a special relation of the subjective feeling and soul of the Poet to the objects of which he sings. His soul, filled with this living glory, is in itself calm, independent, free, self-sufficient, spacious, large; and in this affirmative identity with itself, it expands its life in imagination till it attains to the same calm unity in the Soul of things. And so it coalesces with the objects of Nature and their magnificence, becomes one with the loved one, with the cup-bearer, etc.;—in a word, with all that is worthy of praise and of love, and this in the most blissful and joyous intimacy. The Occidental Romantic inwardness of Soul shews, indeed, a similar consciousness of Life in itself; but on the whole—especially in the North—it is more unhappy, is not free, is given to yearning; or it remains more subjectively shut up in itself, and thereby becomes selfish and sensitive. Such oppressed, disturbed inner states of mind are especially expressed in the National Songs of barbarous peoples. The state of free, joyous inwardness is, on the contrary, characteristic of the Orientals, especially of the Mohammedan Persians, who openly and gladly give up their whole Self to God, as well as to all that is praiseworthy, yet in this very surrender preserve their essential free being, which they can maintain even in relation to the surrounding world. Thus we see in their glow of passion the most expansive blissfulness and outpouring of feeling; and with their inexhaustible wealth of brilliant and magnificent images, through it all there sound the constant tones of happiness, of beauty, and of joy. When the Oriental suffers and is unhappy, he accepts it as the immutable decree of Fate, and in presence of it still remains certain in himself, without becoming depressed, or feeling sensitive, or despondent, or distressed. In the poems of Hafiz we find complaining and repining enough about the loved one, the wine-bringer, etc.; but even in his Pain he remains as free from care as in his Joy. Thus he sings:

> '"Because the Presence of thy Friend
> Is bright, not sad;
> Burn, like the Taper, out in Woe,
> Burn, like the Taper, out in Woe,

'The taper teaches man to laugh and weep; it laughs in bright glances through the flame, although it is melting at the same time in hot tears; even in burning itself out, it sheds a bright glance around. This is the general character of the whole of this Poetry.

'To cite some of their more special images: the Persian Poets speak much of Flowers and Precious Stones, and especially of the Rose and the Nightingale. It is very common for them to represent the Nightingale as the "Bridegroom" of the Rose. This attributing of a Soul to the Rose and of Love to the Nightingale, occurs frequently in Hafiz. "O Rose," he says, "while grateful for being the Sultana of Beauty, vouchsafe not to be proud to the Love of the Nightingale." He speaks himself of the Nightingale of his own Heart. But when we speak in our Poetry of Roses, Nightingales, and Wine, it is done in a quite other and more prosaic sense: the Rose is regarded as for ornament; we are "crowned with Roses"; or we hear the Nightingale and sympathise with it; we drink Wine, and call it the Dispeller of Care. With the Persian Poets, however, the Rose is not an image, or a symbol, or a mere ornament; but it actually appears to the Poet as animated with a Soul, as a loving Bride; and he penetrates with his spirit deep into the Soul of the Rose.'

C. VON HAMMER'S ACCOUNT OF OMAR KHAYYÁM.

Von Hammer's Account of Omar Khayyám is at once so just, so discriminating, and so well-informed that it may prove interesting to our Readers, especially as the work in which it is contained has become rare; and it may help generally to dispel some of the hallucination still prevalent about the 'Astronomer-Poet of Persia':

'Omar Chiam'—as Von Hammer transliterates the name—'is one of the most remarkable Persian Poets; he is unique as regards the irreligious subject-matter of his Poems, so that, so far as we know, there is no other found like him in the whole History of Persian Poetry. He is the Poet of the Freethinkers and of the Jesters at Religion, and in this respect he may be appropriately called the Voltaire of Persian Poetry. It is remarkable too, that in Persia, as elsewhere, Freethinking was the precursor of Mysticism, and that the Age of the deepest Unbelief passed over into that of the greatest Superstition.

'Omar Chiam, born at Nishapur, was one of the greatest Astronomers of his time; he shared the fame of Nassireddin and Ulugbeg. But Astronomy led him not to the knowledge, but to the denial, of the Supreme Being; and he embodied the result of his sceptical meditations in Quatrains, which have become famous under the title: *Rubayat Omar Chiam*. In his youth he was at school with Nisamol-Mulk, who became afterwards the Grand Vizier of Melekshah, and with Hassan Sabbah, the Founder of the Order of the Assassins. In the bloody prescriptions of his Order, Hassan practically sealed the doctrinal Unbelief which Omar Chiam proclaimed in his Verses; and as its Grand master, he sacrificed his old schoolfellow, the Grand Vizier, to his revenge, because he continued to follow the path of Right and Virtue. Omar Chiam, as the friend of Hassan Sabbah, is supposed to have helped him to found his diabolical Doctrine and his diabolical Society.'

So far Von Hammer. We commend his last statement to the serious consideration of the amiable Devotees of the new Red-letter Cult of our fashionable Omar Khayyám Societies and Clubs! The remarks on this subject in our Introduction apply, of course, only to *Fitzgerald's* Omar, of whom he takes a low view—very pithily summed up by himself in this phrase: 'the burden of Omar's Song—if not "Let us eat"—is *assuredly*—"Let us drink, for Tomorrow we die!"' As regards the *real* Omar, whom Mr. Fitzgerald did not rightly understand, our view agrees generally with that of Von Hammer and M. Nicolas, but it need not be discussed here. The phenomenal success of Mr. Fitzgerald's Version in recent years has been largely due to the witchery and glamour of his Versification. His lasting achievement—and it is not a small one—is to have thoroughly popularised the Quatrain. We now hear it echoed everywhere, and in all sorts of connections, even the most trivial. It has recently been applied, with amusing ingenuity, to the Game of Golf, and even to the translation of Homer by Mr. Mackail. But the most deliciously ridiculous thing of the kind in the connection, yet seen, is Baron Corvo's Translation of M. Nicolas—'*Risum teneatis, Amici?*'

These effusions are, after all, only amusing manifestations of the Omar Khayyám Distemper. It has, however, unhappily a deeper significance. Mr. Fitzgerald's success has arisen mainly from his playing into the *pessimistic and cynical mood* of the time, and here lies its moral danger, especially to young, unguarded and unthinking, readers. Let them be assured that all this is bad thought, bad taste, bad effort. The *Byronic* mood is not only unhealthy, but is critically antiquated, and cannot be permanently recalled in any relation whatever. Better—much better—than this is the healthy, if somewhat rabid, physical progression of Mr. Rudyard Kipling, even to 'ride with the reckless seraphim on the brim of a red-maned star'! If they will not take it from us, let them listen to the powerful and earnest words of a lofty, original, spiritual thinker with which he corrected the kindred morbid tendencies of his day, and which are again singularly relevant here. Says Professor Ferrier in a noble and indignant outburst: 'These aberrations betoken a perverse and prurient play of the abnormal fancy—groping for the very holy of holies in kennels running with the most senseless and God-abandoned abominations. Our natural superstitions are bad enough; but thus to make a systematic business of fatuity, imposture, and profanity, and to imagine, all the while, that we are touching on the precincts of God's Spiritual Kingdom, is unspeakably shocking. The horror and disgrace of such proceedings were never even approached in the darkest days of heathendom and idolatry. Ye who make shattered nerves and depraved sensations the interpreters of truth—ye who inaugurate disease as the prophet of all wisdom, thus making sin, death, and the devil, the lords paramount of the creation—have ye bethought yourselves of the backward and downward course which ye are running into the pit of the bestial and the abhorred? Oh, ye miserable mystics! when will ye know that all God's truths and all man's blessings lie in the broad health, in the trodden ways, and in the laughing sunshine of the universe, and that all intellect, all genius, is merely *the power of seeing wonders in common things!'*

With this impressive appeal we pause, for the present. The standpoint and genius of Jeláleddín could not possibly be better expressed than in Ferrier's closing words.

ALSO AVAILABLE

FULL TITLE: The Mesnevi of Mevlānā Jelālu'd-dīn er-Rūmī. *Book first, together with some account of the life and acts of the Author, of his ancestors, and of his descendants, illustrated by a selection of characteristic anedocts, as collected by their historian, Mevlānā Shemsu'd-dīn Ahmed el-Eflākī el-'Arifī, translated and the poetry versified by James W. Redhouse.*

- ISBN PAPER: 9782357287082
- ISBN HARDCOVER: 9782357287099
- ISBN E-BOOK: 9782357287105

The Masnavi I Ma'navi of Rumi

Complete 6 Books

- ISBN PAPER: 9798709722125
- ISBN HARDCOVER: 9782357287136
- ISBN E-BOOK: 9782357287143

JALÁLU'D-DÍN RÚMÍ

Wisdom of the East - The Persian Mystics

- ISBN PAPER: 9798708937155
- ISBN HARDCOVER: 9782357287112
- ISBN E-BOOK: 9782357287129

Copyright © 2021 by Alicia Editions
All rights reserved.

Credit Images: Canva, Wikimedia Commons, by Hanafi-maturidi - Own work, CC BY 3.0, https://commons.wikimedia.org/w/index.php?curid=14844683; A Sufi in Ecstasy in a Landscape. Iran, Isfahan (c. 1650-1660)
No part of this book may be reproduced in any form or by any electronic or mechanical means, including information storage and retrieval systems, without written permission from the author, except for the use of brief quotations in a book review.